RACINE

OR

THE TRIUMPH OF
RELEVANCE

BY

ODETTE DE MOURGUES

*Fellow of Girton College and Lecturer in French
in the University of Cambridge*

CAMBRIDGE
AT THE UNIVERSITY PRESS
1967

Published by the Syndics of the Cambridge University Press
Bentley House, 200 Euston Road, London, N.W. 1
American Branch: 32 East 57th Street, New York, N.Y. 10022

© Cambridge University Press 1967

Library of Congress Catalogue Card Number: 67-11520

Printed in Great Britain
at the University Printing House, Cambridge
(Brooke Crutchley, University Printer)

CONTENTS

iii

PREFACE

This book is intended to help the English reader to a better appreciation of Racine and is based on two assumptions. One is that no study of Racinian tragedy can be completely original. It is inevitable that a number of critics, studying the text with the same patience and care, should on some points have come independently to the same conclusions. I welcome the opportunity of expressing here the pleasure I have experienced in finding myself so often in agreement with some of the most distinguished Anglo-Saxon Racinian specialists, and particularly American scholars. At the present time, when the newcomer finds himself confronted with very divergent views as to the significance and poetic value of Racine's theatre, it is not superfluous to say again, and perhaps more strongly, things which have been said before. This leads to my second assumption: that it is still possible for a twentieth-century reader or spectator to understand and derive great satisfaction from Racinian tragedy as seen in the light of seventeenth-century aesthetics; and, moreover, that this is by far the most rewarding approach.

The limited scope of this study has compelled me to leave out some interesting aspects of Racine's dramatic works, such as the valuable data given by his two earlier tragedies, and to make only some passing references to *Esther*. I hope, however, that the following chapters may encourage the general reader to pursue his exploration of the Racinian universe.

Passages from Racine are quoted from the Pléiade edition—*Racine—Œuvres complètes*, ed. R. Picard, 1950.

O. M.

Cambridge 1966

THE CHOICE OF A FOCUS

I must start with a warning. This book is not intended for those whose sole interest is to acquire or to enlarge a theoretical knowledge of Racine, but for readers whose relationships with Racine's tragedies have been, at some time or other, a first-hand personal experience. As to the nature and scope of such an experience, I can only guess. It may have been a fleeting reaction, half-forgotten before it was properly registered, a sudden impulse, an almost visceral desire to side with Athalie against God, Joas and Joad when, before dying, she utters her desperate cry of hatred: 'Dieu des Juifs, tu l'emportes.' It may have been a moment of infinite pity, an illuminating moment of insight into the hopelessness of human relations, when Pyrrhus, face to face with Hermione, lets slip the unforgivable remark: 'Rien ne vous engageait à m'aimer en effet.' It may perhaps have been at times—while watching Agrippine being defeated by Néron or listening to Phèdre's confession of her love—a strange dryness in the throat as well as an ill-defined but intense satisfaction, a compulsion to cry, not for grief, but as under the spell of some almost transcendental experience.

No one, I think, who is not endowed with the possibility of being violently moved by Racine, emotionally, aesthetically, even before wondering why, can derive any profit from this book, nor, for that matter, from any study of Racinian tragedy. In the same way no amount of reading and analysing would help a reader of Proust who had never experienced personally the shock of recovering a moment of his past through a sensation. On the other hand the reader who knows, through immediate and first-hand knowledge, the kind of experience with which Proust is concerned will, by studying Proust's works, not only enrich his personal outlook on life but also appreciate to the full the aesthetic pattern the novelist wove around this central experience.

Studying Racine is basically to link our immediate emotional responses to his tragedies with an intellectual framework of analyses in order to increase as much as possible the intensity and the complexity of the impact which even a single line of his plays may have on us.

I should not have stressed so heavily what an approach to Racine's tragedies requires from our sensibility if I had not met a number of intelligent people who admitted with great honesty that Racine left them unmoved, although they possessed in theory very sound and very precise notions on the perfection of his tragedies. No aspersion should be cast on anybody who finds himself in a similar case. Aesthetic experiences are of many kinds and Racine is not the only great dramatist in the world.

To be blessed with the right sort of sensibility is not enough, obviously. The aesthetic satisfaction produced by the reading of Racine's tragedies may leave us with the feeling of its being incomplete, or too vague, or of being limited to a particular scene or speech. This is true of all of us. Even after years of reading Racine, one suddenly realizes that a line, read perhaps over a hundred times, had not yielded its complete and perfect significance until that very moment. In the process of appreciating Racine, intellectual analysis and instinctive reactions of our sensibility help each other. The ideal appreciation of Racine is reached when, to borrow an expression from Montaigne, Racine's tragedies are for us 'intellectuellement sensibles, sensiblement intellectuelles'.

This double requirement implies a rather delicate balance in our approach to Racine. The intellectual interpretation may overshoot its target and miss the emotional centre of a scene. The strong emotional response may lead to crude and erroneous explanations.

The most insidious way in which our approach to Racine may be misdirected is through a tempting confusion between art and life. Deeply moved by Racine, we are tempted to account for our emotions in terms of the familiar pattern of ordinary life. We think, for instance, that a writer who presents us with such a disturbing picture of the human condition must have experienced or witnessed devastating passions in the course of his life and that the key to his achievement is to be found in his biography. Or else, because Racinian characters impose on us their unshakable presence, we beckon them to step out of the play so that we may circle round them, examining curiously the idiosyncrasies of their personalities, as we would scrutinize and sum up the human beings we meet in real life. Even the admiration felt for the simplicity and the universality of Racine's plots takes the form, very often, of an analogy with current events, with *faits divers*. These are comparatively naïve reactions before the overwhelming impression of reality given to us by Racine's tragedies. The tendency to look for realistic clues to such an impression may assume more subtle forms. But, in all cases, the result is the same: what has been done is to swell and disfigure the Racinian text with all the raw material which it is precisely the supreme art of Racine to have excluded.

In order to avoid such distortion and to preserve a balanced critical attitude to the works of Racine, the safest starting-point is to consider what kind of literary production these works are and what general aesthetic purpose is implied in the particular genre chosen by the writer.

Racine's plays are tragedies. As such they belong to a tradition we all know and which includes, among others, the Greek Dramatists, Shakespeare and Corneille.

Many books have been written on what this literary genre, tragedy, represents in our Western tradition. Without going into a lengthy historical survey, one may agree on a certain number of comparatively simple features which characterize what we call a tragedy.

The origins of tragedy are a little obscure but the first enacted works of drama which could be given the name, such as the Passion Plays of Egypt or Syria, contains the essential element of tragedy. A hero, who is a sort of superman—mythological, semi-historical or ancestral—is defeated by a superior antagonist; he suffers, dies and is born again. This pattern corresponds undoubtedly to something very basic in man: an instinctive terror of the superior forces which are a threat to humanity, nature, fate or gods; a wish to oppose them with a magnified image of man, a desire to establish a pattern of order. This order is represented in the primitive play by the pattern of the cycle of death and rebirth and by the ritualistic character of a play conceived as a religious ceremony with solemn and formal gestures.

We have here all the ingredients of the tragedies we know: the magnified image of man, the hero being larger than life-size either because of personal qualities, or by his divine origin, or for social reasons; the opposing forces, which can be the gods, fate, or political circumstances; the catastrophic clash, always on an impressive scale, involving suffering and sometimes death; whatever the ending, which is generally unhappy but not necessarily so, the indication of some transcendental order; finally the ritualistic element, the enacting of this conflict being a kind of ceremony and the formal aspect of it satisfying originally a religious emotion which in more modern times becomes an aesthetic emotion.

Although all these elements are always present in any tragedy, the form they take varies according to the civilization of the age. For instance, in Shakespeare the opposing forces destroying man are vast, almost cosmic, forces like the pressure of war or the imminence of chaos, whereas in Racine destruction operates through passions within the heart of man. The tragic conflict, as well as the suggested order, reflects the moral and even political climate of the age: order in Sophocles and Euripides refers to a pagan conception of man, whereas in Corneille and Racine it is linked with Christian views on the human condition. The ritualistic shape of a tragedy which presupposes that the audience participates in a kind of sacred ceremony again varies with the customs and tastes of the audience. This accounts for the importance of the chorus in Greek tragedy, the frequency of wrestling matches and duels in Shakespeare, and the fact that Racinian tragedy has been described as a high mass celebrated to the glory of the Sun King.

These different forms of tragedy did not exist separately; each one influenced the dramatists who came after. Corneille and Racine were intensely conscious of the tradition of great tragedies they had behind them: the Greeks, Seneca, the sixteenth-century dramatists like Garnier. They also belonged to an age which since the Renaissance had studied very closely the technical aspects of tragedy, as witness the numerous theoretical treatises on drama written during two centuries. Both of them faced the same problem: how to take into account a respected and precious tradition and yet create their own variety of tragedy in keeping with the preoccupations, tastes and sensibility of their age. They both succeeded in outstanding ways. The solution to the problem was of course different for each of them; even without any mention of differences in their personality as writers, they belonged to different moments in the century. It is comparatively easy to realize the originality of Corneille as well as to be aware of his intense efforts to recreate tragedy: the bulk and variety of his works, the importance of his critical writings, the contradictory judgments on him are a constant challenge to critics and students of his plays. The originality of Racine is unobtrusive, taken for granted. His theoretical writings, limited to prefaces written after he had written the plays, although they contain interesting statements, do not illuminate the efforts of the creative artist to a very great degree. The main evidence of Racine's original modification of traditional tragedy is to be found in the text of his eight masterpieces.

It would seem, therefore, that the best way to approach Racine's individual greatness as a tragic dramatist is to analyse the particular way in which he deals with the essential elements of the tragedy: the tragic hero, the opposing forces, the clash, the outcome, order and ceremony. The drawback of such a piecemeal analysis is obvious. A tragedy forms a united whole. In lesser dramatists the various elements may not be very well fused; for instance, the ritualistic framework may hide or blur the clash between the hero and the forces which destroy him. In a great dramatist the fusion between the different elements should be as complete as possible. And this fusion is directed towards a definite purpose: that of producing the intense emotion I mentioned at the beginning of this chapter. The emotion produced by tragedy has always been recognized as being of a particular kind and is usually described as being a mixture of fear and pity. It is a convenient description and roughly accurate. From what we have seen of the general features of tragedy, fear of a superior force antagonistic to man and sympathy for the hero who stands for humanity are obviously part of the essence of the genre. It should be kept in mind, however, that the description, while stressing the fundamental reactions of our sensibility, leaves out a whole range of emotional harmonics.[1]

Perhaps of all the tragic dramatists who have successfully striven towards the perfect fusion of all the elements which constitute a tragedy, Racine is the one who has come nearest to an absolute perfection.

Everything in his tragedies is directed towards one single

[1] See chapter 7.

aim: to bring the tragic emotion to the highest degree of intensity; this intensity depends on both the singleness of purpose and the complexity of the technique. I say complexity although it is usual to praise in Racine an extreme simplicity in the elements of his dramatic technique. The elements, it is true, are simple in themselves, such as a single action lasting twenty-four hours, a vocabulary which may appear to some as seventeenth-century basic French. But the secret of Racine's greatness does not lie in this much praised simplicity. What is important in his plays is not the various elements: characterization, plot or language, as such, but their function. Because of this function, the same one, common to them all—the intensifying of the tragic emotion—, they compose a very complicated network of interactions which alters them considerably. What we conceived as simple because they were well within the elementary range of our imagination—the unity of place, feelings which are universal, ordinary words—become parts of an autonomous world which dictates their significance, their degree of stylization, the scope of their importance.

The purpose of this study is to examine not so much the components of Racinian tragedy as some of the patterns created by their interdependence and their common function. When we consider these patterns, we may see that simplicity and complexity are not very good criteria by which to judge the artistic achievement of Racine. Stylization, which is a simplifying process, and paradox, which is a complex synthesis, are equally used by the dramatist when they serve his purpose. In fact the most striking aspect of Racine's art—the one this book wants to emphasize—might be described as the triumph of relevance.

2

THE MULTIVALENCY OF
TIME AND SPACE

There is no theatre without dramatic conventions, since a play is never a faithful copy of reality. Even the most realistic kind of play—the slice-of-life type—follows some arbitrary rules. And the less realistic the theatre, the more and the stricter the conventions.

They consist of a stylization of reality which is convenient dramatically and, as such, they vary with the kind of drama the playwright intends to write. Also, as they imply a tacit agreement between the writer and his audience, they must be easily grasped and therefore in keeping with contemporary tastes and habits of mind. In Elizabethan drama the theme of error, of mistaken identity, played an important part; hence the convention of disguise: as soon as a character changed his clothes and called himself by another name, not even his own parents could recognize him. An Elizabethan audience expected to witness a good fight on the stage and perhaps to see their favourite wrestlers appear in the course of the play; accordingly, the duel became to a certain extent a conventional feature of plays, was used by the playwright to increase the dramatic intensity and occupied a key position in some tragedies.

Yet many people tend to think of dramatic conventions as tiresome rules which are a hindrance to the dramatist but which he must observe in order to conform to some literary ideal dictated from outside. This opinion is particularly deep-rooted in the case of French classicism. The mention of the three unities, of the *bienséances*, etc., seems to awake an instinctive feeling of pity for Corneille and Racine and a tendency to assess their achievement in terms of *la difficulté vaincue*. This is a misconception of the nature of dramatic conventions, which exist to help the dramatist, not to hinder him. If they prove unhelpful or anachronistic, he can question or modify them. Corneille, for instance, who never took any point of dramatic technique for granted, indulged in a thorough critical examination of the unities.

Critics have never ceased marvelling at the ease and elegant naturalness with which Racine unobtrusively complies with the requirements of contemporary dramatic conventions. But it is not enough to say that Racine gives the impression that the observance of the rules created no problem for him. Dramatic conventions play a positive part in his tragedies: they are precious tools used to increase tragic intensity. We shall find them in the following chapters as relevant elements of the dramatic patterns.

The arbitrary simplification of reality imposed by the conventions leads in Racinian tragedy to a very subtle and complex treatment of the side of the reality which has been thus stylized. As a first illustration, nothing is more illuminating than Racine's use of time and space, in keeping with the rule of the unities.[1]

★

The rule according to which the dramatic action was not to take more than twenty-four hours was based on a care for verisimilitude. The theatrical illusion, that is, the illusion of witnessing real events, seemed easier to obtain if there was not too wide a difference between the actual performance of the play and the probable duration of the events represented on the stage.

One's attention tends to focus on the dramatist's difficulty in finding events which could be compressed within the twenty-four hour period, and Racine is praised for having chosen a type of plot based on psychological events, which escape the

[1] This point has been treated in J. C. Lapp's most interesting book, *Aspects of Racinian Tragedy* (Toronto, 1956), ch. II, and I shall refer to some of his illuminating comments in the course of this chapter.

material measurements of time. But this is the wrong approach to Racine's use of the convention of time. To begin with, it is not very accurate. If some of his tragedies have very few striking incidents (such as *Bérénice*), this is not true of *Britannicus* or of *Bajazet*. It is also to dismiss rather rashly the time element in psychological reactions, whereas the relations between time and human sensibility are very important in Racinian tragedy.

The best way to approach the rule of the twenty-four hours is to stop thinking in terms of ordinary duration, measured by the clock. The convention does not compel Racine to a realistic copy of a twenty-four hour period. It operates a radical change in the nature of time. The essential point of the rule is that ordinary time is replaced by conventional time, 'ideal' time, possessing attributes of its own, and particularly an extreme elasticity. Time in Racine constantly fluctuates in length, in keeping with the necessities of dramatic intensity.

The arbitrary length of time chosen by the convention implies shortness and thus gives the impression of the immediate present. Racine frequently increases this effect of short duration. The present becomes one single moment, a supremely important moment, cut off from the web of duration.

It is often the moment when the decision taken or to be taken is of such importance that it obliterates everything else and puts an end to all calculations of time. Racinian characters are clearly aware of the terrifying finality of the moment and the expression *pour la dernière fois*, which recurs many times in the theatre of Racine, underlines the intense tragic value of the irretrievable moment. It may be coloured by the tone of a veiled threat:

Pour la dernière fois je vous parle peut-être,   (IV, v)

says Hermione to Pyrrhus, or by that of an openly menacing command, as with Mithridate's injunction to Monime that she should banish Xipharès from her thoughts:

Profitez du moment que mon amour vous donne:
Pour la dernière fois, venez, je vous l'ordonne.   (IV, iv)

It may be also the ultimate moment which precedes the complete annihilation of the hero, with the full consciousness of his imminent destruction. Thus in *Bérénice* the three characters, in the last act, express with the same words the feeling of having reached either the extreme limit of their strength:

TITUS (*to Antiochus*)   Venez, Prince, venez. Je veux bien que vous même
Pour la dernière fois vous voyiez si je l'aime;   (v, iii)

or the tragic acceptance of their fate:

Pour la dernière fois je me suis consulté;   (v, vii)

says Antiochus; and Bérénice's last words take up again the knell-like statement of despair:

Pour la dernière fois, adieu, Seigneur.   (v, vii)

But Racine's focusing of time into moments to give an intense relief to a particular climax is not the only way in which the unit of the moment is used to intensify our tragic emotion.

Moments in Racine are not of equal duration. In a play like *Bajazet* the brevity, the scarcity of moments, is emphasized, since in that tragedy the tragic pattern is centred on Roxane's relentless pursuit of Bajazet and on the characters' precarious hold on existence. From Act I we know that Roxane expects Bajazet to make a decision that very day, *dans cette journée*, and that if he refuses to marry her:

Dès le même moment, sans songer si je l'aime
......
J'abandonne l'ingrat.   (I, iii)

It is an integral part of the play that none of the characters can afford any time to hesitate and consider; any delay is fraught with danger and we are constantly reminded of the pressing orders of the absent Sultan. Hence the feeling of feverish hurry which seizes Roxane:

> Le temps presse. Que faire en ce doute funeste?
> Allons: employons bien le moment qui nous reste. (III, viii)

and even affects Acomat:

> Ne tardons plus, marchons. (IV, vii)

The last act shows an alarming acceleration of time. Roxane's reference to *moments* reaches a despairing and sinister frenzy in her last conversation with Bajazet:

> Les moments sont trop chers pour les perdre en paroles.
> ......
> Laissons ces vains discours; et sans m'importuner,
> Pour la dernière fois, veux-tu vivre et régner?
> J'ai l'ordre d'Amurat et je puis t'y soustraire.
> Mais tu n'as qu'un moment. Parle. (v, iv)

In *Bérénice*, on the contrary, moments are loaded with tragic implications for the opposite reason; their unendurable length. Time in that tragedy is a terrifying element because it passes too slowly. Waiting for Titus' decision is a torture for Bérénice:

> Phénice ne vient point? Moments trop rigoureux,
> Que vous paraissez lents à mes rapides vœux! (IV, i)

This deliberate stretching of each moment is part of a larger pattern, which I shall mention later; for *Bérénice* is the tragedy of absence—remembered, experienced and still to come. As far as the present is concerned, this slowing down of the passing of time gives to moments a cruel power of expansion and their dramatic intensity is derived from their quality of never-ending suffering and the succession of conflicting moods they contain, a paradox forcefully expressed by Antiochus in Act v, scene v:

> Tous mes moments ne sont qu'un éternel passage
> De la crainte à l'espoir, de l'espoir à la rage.

Phèdre presents us with yet another use by Racine of the moment. In spite of the occurrence of a certain number of events in the course of the play, we have the impression that

Phèdre's fate is contained in one moment. She appears in the first act, ready for death:

> Je ne me soutiens plus, ma force m'abandonne.
> Mes yeux sont éblouis du jour que je revois
> ......
> Soleil, je viens te voir pour la dernière fois. (I, iii)

Her last words express the same feelings, the same dazzled worship of light:

> Déjà je ne vois plus qu'à travers un nuage
> Et le ciel, et l'époux que ma présence outrage;
> Et la mort, à mes yeux dérobant la clarté,
> Rend au jour qu'ils souillaient toute sa pureté. (v, vii)

This juxtaposition of two moments in Phèdre's ordeal, the identity of the first with the last, is not only extremely beautiful architecturally in the general structure of the play, but also intensifies to the extreme the tragic quality of inescapability in Phèdre's fate.

On the other hand, though Phèdre's tragedy, which is that of one moment, lasts for five acts, Hippolyte's final destruction, which implies a succession of actions, occurs with brutal rapidity.[1]

It is a characteristic of the 'ideal' time of Racinian tragedy that the pace, the tempo, is modified considerably, even within the same play, and always in the way which is relevant to the intensifying of the tragic emotion.

[1] Jean Pommier calculates that the events narrated by Théramène in the *récit* of the death of Hippolyte do not have time to happen: 'Le départ d'Hippolyte, la rencontre du monstre, le combat et ses épisodes, la mort du héros, le retour du messager, il faut que tout cela se passe dans un temps record, le temps de dire soixante-dix vers: quelque chose comme quatre minutes et quart' (*Aspects de Racine*, Paris, 1954, p. 200). The arithmetical precision of these figures relates of course to our measurement of ordinary time and therefore the objection is irrelevant. The rapid fulfilment of Thésée's prayer to Neptune and the leisurely narration of Hippolyte's fight with the monster belong to two different aspects of the event, and the duration of each, according to 'ideal' time, is measured differently in keeping with their respective tragic import.

This elasticity of Racinian time does not account only for the subtle ways in which time shrinks or expands in the present. It also accounts for the perfect integration of the past and the future in the tragedy.

Undoubtedly the immediate past must be revealed as soon as possible, in order that we may grasp at once the external event which starts the mechanism of the play. In that respect Racine's exposition scenes have been rightly admired. What is interesting to note here is how almost imperceptible is the joint between the present and the events which precede.

In *Iphigénie* when the play begins it is still dusk. Everything is quiet and motionless:

> Mais tout dort, et l'armée, et les vents et Neptune. (i, i)

This lull of the early morning is still part of the disheartening lull which, we are told afterwards, has lasted for three months.

Agrippine's agitation at the beginning of *Britannicus*, mentioned in the first lines by her confidante,

> Quoi! tandis que Néron s'abandonne au sommeil,
> Faut-il que vous veniez attendre son réveil?
> Qu'errant dans le palais sans suite et sans escorte, (i, i)

is connected with the atmosphere of unrest already pervading the palace and with the disorderly events which have happened during the night, and has the added ironical value of the reference to Néron's sleep. Néron has not slept that night.

Past events which have affected the present mood of a character are also made a part of the present because the character who narrates them relives them, so to speak, as he talks. Professor Lapp's close study of Oreste's evocation of the past in the first scene of *Andromaque* shows how Racine produces the effect of simultaneity of events by a subtle juxtaposition of the past definite and present indicative tenses.[1] The result is not only to juxtapose different moments in the past but also to indicate that

---

[1] *Aspects of Racinian Tragedy*, pp. 42–44.

this past is still alive in Oreste and that the passion which flares up through the narrative is the same passion as is now consuming him.

Athalie's dream of a few days before still colours her present mood, and her thoughts are still framed by the horrifying darkness of that fatal night:

> Mais un trouble importun vient depuis quelques jours
> De mes prospérités interrompre le cours.
> Un songe (me devrais-je inquiéter d'un songe?)
> Entretient dans mon cœur un chagrin qui le ronge.
> Je l'évite partout, partout il me poursuit.
> C'était pendant l'horreur d'une profonde nuit.   (II, v)

The recalling of past events is particularly interesting when it affects the relationships between passion and time. Fundamentally, as we shall see, Racinian passion is outside time. Unchanged by duration, it remains at the same pitch of intensity, without growth or decline, without beginning or end. And yet, paradoxically, the starting-point of the passion as well as some notion of the time it has lasted are given to us whenever some features in the past history of that passion can emphasize its tragic nature.

Thus the violence of Phèdre's reactions at the first sight of Hippolyte indicates a deliberate and powerful intervention of Venus. Only the wrath of a goddess could with such brutality set aflame the human flesh and heart:

> Je le vis, je rougis, je pâlis à sa vue;
> Un trouble s'éleva dans mon âme éperdue;
> Mes yeux ne voyaient plus, je ne pouvais parler;
> Je sentis tout mon corps et transir et brûler.
> Je reconnus Vénus et ses feux redoutables.   (I, iv)

It is significant that Eriphile should have fallen in love with Achille's face, which, before she looked at him, she had considered awesome and hateful. This sudden shift is in keeping with the characteristics of contradiction and ambiguity in her position towards the other characters, particularly Iphigénie, and of the fate which brings her death.

We are sometimes told, with exact figures, how long a passion has lasted before the play begins. Antiochus has loved Bérénice for five years, a very long time in a tragedy where time drags on so slowly. Bajazet and Atalide have loved each other since childhood; hence the feeling we have of a tough and yet vulnerable alliance in a dangerous world; and this increases the tragic quality of Atalide's suspicions and of Roxane's cruel blackmail.

In *Mithridate*, the first meeting of Xipharès and Monime, related by Xipharès, is pushed back into a delicately hazy past, as the young man, for fear of displeasing Monime, whose feelings he does not know, recalls the beginning of his love for her, in a gentle, apologetic tone:

> Ne vous souvient-il plus, en quittant vos beaux yeux,
> Quelle vive douleur attendrit mes adieux?
> Je m'en souviens tout seul. Avouez-le, Madame,
> Je vous rappelle un songe effacé de votre âme.   (I, ii)

This kind of subtle delicacy, this aura of shyness around passion, is a distinctive feature of Xipharès and Monime.

In the case of Oreste, whose personality in the tragedy is focused towards an irrational murder, it is important that his melancholy, his helplessness and hopelessness, should be given the enlargement of the past:

> Tu vis mon désespoir et tu m'as vu depuis
> Traîner de mers en mers ma chaîne et mes ennuis.   (I, i)

> J'ai mendié la mort chez des peuples cruels,   (II, ii)

the enlargement of past time being accentuated by the suggestions of sea voyages and far-off countries.

The past actions of a character can be relevant to his present tragic position. Néron's 'trois ans de vertus', so often mentioned in the play, and Agrippine's criminal acts which secured the throne for Néron, lengthily and ambiguously recalled in Act IV, are an intrinsic part of the two characters' present fate and of their complex and tragic relationships.

Allusions to past events vary in number according to their relevance to the general pattern. *Andromaque* represents an extreme case of the importance given to the past: the obsession with the Trojan war affects not only Andromaque herself, who constantly relives

> ...cette nuit cruelle
> Qui fut pour tout un peuple une nuit éternelle.   (III, viii)

not only Pyrrhus, for whom Troy in ruins is still a vivid picture seen in the present:

> Je ne vois que des tours que la cendre a couvertes,
> Un fleuve teint de sang, des campagnes désertes,   (I, ii)

and whose devouring love for Andromaque is inextricably fused with the part he played in the defeat of Troy:

> Brûlé de plus de feux que je n'en allumai.   (II, i)

even Oreste and Hermione refer to Troy; Oreste suggests a re-enacting of the terrible war:

> Hé bien! allons, Madame:
> Mettons encore un coup toute la Grèce en flamme;
> Prenons, en signalant mon bras et votre nom,
> Vous la place d'Hélène, et moi, d'Agamemnon.   (IV, iii)

Hermione has not forgotten the power her mother had of starting the war, and (in Act V, scene ii) compares bitterly her own helplessness with Hélène's terrifying sway over the lives of all the Greeks.

This obsessive conjuring up of Troy is obviously central to the relations between Pyrrhus and Andromaque. But it is not only important in the tragic pattern of the play; we shall see later that Troy plays a symbolic part, and stands for certain values which triumph at the end of the tragedy.

The expansion of the present into the past is also motivated by the very nature of the tragic hero, who must be a magnified image of man. One way of enlarging his stature is to connect him with an impressive historical or legendary past. Thus Mithridate's tragic personality is largely built on 'les quarante ans de lutte' with Rome; and Phèdre, 'la fille de Minos et de Pasiphaé', is so near the legendary past that she moves in a world where 'le père et le maître des dieux' is her 'aïeul' and the supreme judge of the underworld is her own father.

References to the past are also a means of giving temporal depth to the superior forces which destroy the hero. Phèdre's family history shows the persistence and increased violence of Vénus' persecution:

> Puisque Vénus le veut, de ce sang déplorable
> Je péris la dernière, et la plus misérable.　　(ɪ, iii)

In *Iphigénie* the present tragic fate which tears apart Agamemnon's family stretches back to past family tragedies. In the quarrel scene between Agamemnon and Clytemnestre, the latter recalls the horrible legendary story of Agamemnon's father Atreus who set for food before his brother Thyestes the flesh of his own son:

> Vous ne démentez point une race funeste.
> Oui, vous êtes le sang d'Atrée et de Thyeste,
> Bourreau de votre fille, il ne vous reste enfin
> Que d'en faire à sa mère un horrible festin.　　(ɪv, iv)

Ideal time becomes such a fluid and docile element through the skill of the playwright that the same speech, the same mood in a character, may include past, present and even future. Néron's speech is a relation of a past event and past emotions:

> 　　　Excité d'un désir curieux,
> Cette nuit je l'ai vue arriver en ces lieux,
> Triste, levant au ciel ses yeux mouillés de larmes,
> Qui brillaient au travers des flambeaux et des armes:
> Belle, sans ornements, dans le simple appareil
> D'une beauté qu'on vient d'arracher au sommeil.

Que veux-tu? Je ne sais si cette négligence,
Les ombres, les flambeaux, les cris et le silence,
Et le farouche aspect de ses fiers ravisseurs
Relevaient de ses yeux les timides douceurs.
Quoi qu'il en soit, ravi d'une si belle vue,
J'ai voulu lui parler, et ma voix s'est perdue:
Immobile, saisi d'un long étonnement,
Je l'ai laissé passer dans son appartement.
J'ai passé dans le mien. C'est là que solitaire,
De son image en vain j'ai voulu me distraire:
Trop présente à mes yeux, je croyais lui parler;
J'aimais jusqu'à ses pleurs que je faisais couler.
Quelquefois, mais trop tard, je lui demandais grâce;
J'employais les soupirs, et même la menace.
Voilà comme, occupé de mon nouvel amour,
Mes yeux, sans se fermer, ont attendu le jour.
Mais je m'en fais peut-être une trop belle image;
Elle m'est apparue avec trop d'avantage:
Narcisse, qu'en dis-tu?

But the emotion of wonder experienced in the preceding night:

> Immobile, saisi d'un long étonnement,

still lingers in the present, mixed with the conceit of the critical aesthete:

> Mais je m'en fais peut-être une trop belle image.

This tone of complacency is subtly indicated from the beginning of the speech, in the '...Je ne sais si cette négligence...'. The genuine passion which has been born in the heart of Néron assumes particular nuances. The conjuring up of the timid girl surrounded by brutal soldiers, a picture in contrasts, seems to appeal not only to Néron's aesthetic sense but also to a strain of sadism in him. The ambiguity of the line

> J'aimais jusqu'à ces pleurs que je faisais couler,

which implies both the all-embracing passion and the touch of cruelty, confirms the suggestion of a future Néron deriving an aesthetic and sadistic pleasure from the burning of Rome. The fusion of past, present and future is thus done with great economy and a careful balance. This temporal element gives to the speech a multidimensional quality and reveals an alarming complexity in Néron's love for Junie.

The part played by the future is as important in Racinian tragedy as that played by the past, and here again the inclusion of the future within the present is admirably calculated according to its relevance to the tragic centre of each play.

The tragic intensity of Néron's first murder is made more sinister by an intimation of his future crimes, and the horror of the duel with his mother is intensified by her prediction:

> Je prévois que tes coups viendront jusqu'à ta mère. (v, v)

There are cases where it is not even necessary for Racine to mention a future happening. He can rely on the fact that the audience is familiar with the story. While we watch the terrible quarrel between Agamemnon and Clytemnestre, every word of hatred in Clytemnestre's mouth suggests to us the inevitable outcome of their relationship.

At times the vista opened up into the future is made more tragic through dramatic irony. Such is the case in the little Joas' prayer at the end of *Athalie*:

> Dieu, . . .
> . . . . . .
> Faites que Joas meure avant qu'il vous oublie,   (v, vii)

which we know is vain; or in Iphigénie's mention of her brother Oreste when she tries to comfort her mother:

> Vos yeux me reverront dans Oreste mon frère.
> Puisse-t-il être, hélas, moins funeste à sa mère !   (v, iii)

In some of the tragedies the part played by the future is particularly emphasized, and for different purposes.

Whereas in *Andromaque* all the characters were constantly looking back to the past, *Bérénice* is marked by an obsession with the future. Separation and absence are the outcome of the tragedy, and are foreseen and dreaded by the three heroes throughout the play.

Two sides of the future are stressed. One is the repeated assertion that no lapse of time will alter the characters' feelings: the present will live on for ever in the future. Bérénice is and will always be *présente* in Titus' mind:

BERENICE Mais parliez-vous de moi quand je vous ai surpris?
    Dans vos secrets discours étais-je interessée,
    Seigneur? Etais-je au moins présente à la pensée?
TITUS N'en doutez point, Madame, et j'atteste les Dieux
    Que toujours Bérénice est présente à mes yeux.
    L'absence ni le temps, je vous le jure encore,
    Ne vous peuvent ravir ce cœur qui vous adore. (II, v)

Titus' love is expressed even more strongly in Act III, scene i, at the end of his long speech to Antiochus:

    Adieu: ne quittez point ma princesse, ma reine,
    Tout ce qui de mon cœur fut l'unique désir,
    Tout ce que j'aimerai jusqu'au dernier soupir.

The formal rhetorical pattern of this final couplet welds into a powerful statement the acknowledgement of his passion, now doomed, and the certainty of its durability. The deliberate hiatus in time between definite past (*fut*) and future (*j'aimerai*) not only suggests that for Titus, dramatically poised between past hopes and future despair, the present is obliterated; it also gives to the lifelong feelings he foresees the same quality of reality and obviousness as that possessed by feelings already fully experienced.

As an ironical contrast, Antiochus' confidant, Arsace, displays a mistaken faith in the power of time, in the effect of absence:

Laissez à ce torrent le temps de s'écouler.
Dans huit jours, dans un mois, n'importe, il faut qu'il passe; (III, iv)

for days and months have a very different value for the three heroes. The future will not bring any change in the cruel intensity of passion. On the other hand, and this is the second aspect of the future in the play, it will drag on at an unendurably slow pace. Titus faces the perspective of a soulless existence, still prolonged by the perverse will of the gods:

> Mon règne ne sera qu'un long bannissement,
> Si le ciel, non content de me l'avoir ravie,
> Veut encore m'affliger par une longue vie. (II, i)

Bérénice experiences, beforehand, the despairing duration of days and months of absence, and their hopeless succession:

> Dans un mois, dans un an, comment souffrirons-nous,
> Seigneur, que tant de mers me séparent de vous?
> Que le jour recommence et que le jour finisse
> Sans que jamais Titus puisse voir Bérénice,
> Sans que de tout le jour je puisse voir Titus! (IV, v)

In *Athalie* the future is cast back into the present for a different reason. The balance of the play requires a clear indication of a Christian order justifying the ways of God and the actions of Joad. Therefore the chorus expresses religious feelings which are more in keeping with the Gospel than with the Old Testament, and Joad's prophetic intimations of the birth of Christ range over centuries:

> Mes yeux s'ouvrent,
> Et les siècles obscurs devant moi se découvrent. (III, vii)

On the contrary, it is part of the particular nature of the tragic in *Bajazet* that the future is annihilated at the same time as the characters. I have mentioned the terrifying acceleration of time near the end of the play. By the end, all possible calculations of time disappear in the rapid, almost simultaneous, destruction of the characters. The future itself is included in the final holocaust.

An interesting use of the future is to be found in *Mithridate*, where its tragic value lies in the fact that it is illusory. Mithridate's plans for the immediate future—his marriage to Monime—

> Aujourd'hui votre époux. Il faut partir demain. (II, iv)

or his orders to Pharnace:

> Les vaisseaux sont tout prêts....
>
> ......
>
> Allez;... (III, i)

will not be carried out. Even more impressive is the illusion of a future campaign against Rome, the magnificent and ambitious plan which he reveals to his sons in scene i of Act III:

> Brûlons ce Capitole où j'étais attendu.
> Détruisons ses honneurs et faisons disparaître
> La honte de cent rois, et la mienne peut-être;
> Et la flamme à la main effaçons tous ces noms
> Que Rome y consacrait à d'éternels affronts.

This great dream, based on remarkable foresight,

> Jamais on ne vaincra les Romains que dans Rome,

brings into the present the future destruction of Rome, and increases the tragic fate of the great conqueror and fighter who is to be cheated of this supreme endeavour and will die miserably through the mutiny of his son.

Illustrations of the versatility of the function of the time element in Racine could easily be multiplied. They all reveal what a precious asset Racine found in the unity of time, in the twenty-four hour rule. The shortness of the conventional span was used for effects of focusing and concentration which increase the tragic predicament of the characters. Because of the rule, events preceding or following the short duration of the action have to be present indirectly and thus to be closely integrated in the dramatic present. The result is a remarkable range in the temporal dimensions, with Racine taking full advantage of the most useful quality of ideal time, its elasticity. We experience the overwhelming importance and urgency of moments, the weight of months and years, the vision of centuries. Time shrinks or expands and also, paradoxically, is abolished altogether.

★

23

The convention of the unity of place is used by Racine in a similar way and contributes to an effect of focusing as well as to a rich complexity.

In a way the place chosen has no real existence, in the ordinary meaning of the word, but only an ideal, symbolic existence, like the drawing-room which stands for hell in Sartre's *Huis-Clos*. Its only *raison d'être* seems to be that human beings should be thrown together, to torture one another without any possible escape.

This impression of claustrophobia is particularly emphasized by Racine in *Britannicus*, *Bajazet* and *Athalie*. Néron's palace and the seraglio in *Bajazet* are prisons and traps into which the characters are lured. Junie and Britannicus are lost as soon as they are in Néron's palace; Athalie's defeat and death are the direct result of having risked herself in the temple.

In *Britannicus* the uneasy feeling of being shut in is made more acute by the knowledge of hidden enemies lurking behind doors or walls. Néron watches Junie's arrival in the palace; later he warns her that 'caché près de ces lieux' he will be present at her conversation with Britannicus. Agrippine anxiously waits near the door of Néron's palace. References are made to other places where people keep spying and scheming, such as the Council Room of the Senate, where Agrippine used to watch the proceedings hidden behind a curtain, or the house of Pallas, where plotters meet. Every room, every hanging, every wall in the palace may conceal danger:

> Ces murs mêmes, Seigneur, peuvent avoir des yeux,
>
> (III, vi)

says Junie to Britannicus.

Evil in the play assumes the particular feature of being treacherously invisible, suffusing the atmosphere with suspicion and dissimulation. Now and then a brutal reaction from Néron brings into the open the visible reality of the guards who are ready to seize Britannicus, or to keep watch on Junie and even

Agrippine. But as a rule the cruel manœuvres are carried out under some kind of disguise. Narcisse pretends to be Britannicus' only friend. Néron displays affectionate feelings towards his mother and even towards Britannicus:

> J'embrasse mon rival mais c'est pour l'étouffer.   (IV, iii)

The murder of Britannicus is in keeping with the sinister secretiveness which seems to ooze from the very walls of the palace:

> Ce dessein s'est conduit avec plus de mystère.   (V, v)

In *Bajazet*, the words 'murs' and 'portes' recur throughout the play. The immediate reality of the prison atmosphere is, moreover, stressed by the mention of another world outside, a world of freedom represented by the sea. Acomat alludes to the ships waiting and ready for his flight. But, except for Acomat, no door in *Bajazet* opens towards the outside. Doors can only open on death, hence the intense tragic effect of Roxane's last word to Bajazet: 'Sortez.'

The symbolic value of the temple in *Athalie* is given the support of strong local colour, much more marked than in any other Racinian tragedy. The songs of the chorus, the presence of the Levites, the allusions to religious rites, to sacrifices, to the child's 'long habit de lin' give a solid reality to the place chosen for the action. It is a formidable place, sacred, dangerous through the efficiency with which it is ruled, oppressive through a kind of thickness in the air where strains of solemn music mix with the heavy perfume of incense—a relevant setting for a barbaric God waiting for his 'proie'.

In contrast the 'cabinet' where the action of *Bérénice* takes place, in between Titus' rooms and those of Bérénice, is curiously empty, a 'lieu de passage', the symbol of a dilemma, of a momentary hesitation between two possible directions. It suggests the precarious shelter the characters have for their private lives. What counts most in the play is not space within, but space without. As was the case with time, Racinian space, which shrinks into a very limited expanse, as in *Athalie*, can be enlarged to include vast territories. In *Bérénice*, the walls of Titus' 'cabinet' are transparent screens letting in immense vistas. Just outside, constantly present, stands Rome, awaiting Titus' decision, Rome, which can enhance its magnificent presence through the most dazzling spectacles:

> De cette nuit, Phénice, as-tu vu la splendeur?
> . . . . . .
> Ces flambeaux, ce bûcher, cette nuit enflammée,
> Ces aigles, ces faisceaux, ce peuple, cette armée,
> Cette foule de rois, ces consuls, ce sénat,
> . . . . . .
> Cette pourpre, cet or,. . . (I, v)

And constantly present also is the Roman Empire—that is, the whole world. 'Univers' is a key word in the play; Titus is 'chéri de l'univers', 'maître de l'univers'; 'tout l'univers fléchit à vos genoux,' says Bérénice to him, and it is against this ever-present backcloth of the universe that the final decision will be taken:

> Servons tous trois d'exemple à l'univers. (v, vii)

Titus' responsibility towards the universe is at the very centre of the tragic conflict. Another central aspect of the tragedy is also made more intensely tragic by these vistas into vast and distant countries. It is the tragedy of absence and of solitude linked with repeated mention of that vague exotic geographical term 'l'Orient', the imprecision of the term accentuating the size and the outlandish character of this setting for loneliness.

The confidant, Paulin, in Act II, scene ii, alludes to the solitude of Cléopatre abandoned by César who

> Seule dans l'Orient la laissa soupirer;

and Antiochus conjurs up in a similar way his memories of Bérénice's absence:

> Dans l'Orient désert quel devint mon ennui!   (I, iv)

When Bérénice imagines the tortures of her separation from Titus, to the terrifying stretch of time she adds the no-less terrifying stretch of distance between them:

> Dans un mois, dans un an, comment souffrirons-nous,
> Seigneur, que tant de mers me séparent de vous?   (IV, v)

The expansion of time and that of space are also used concurrently in *Mithridate* to increase the stature of the hero. Mithridate is not only made great by his years of struggle against Rome but also by the geographical extent of his past conquests:

> ...l'Orient tout plein de ses exploits   (I, iv)

> Et des rives de Pont aux rives du Bosphore,
> Tout reconnut mon père,...   (I, i)

The spatial enlargement of Mithridate's sphere of activity is particularly impressive in Act III, scene i, when Mithridate recapitulates his past actions and plans his future campaign. Pharnace and Xipharès, each in turn, while expressing opposing opinions, conjure up the vision of a kingdom extending from the rising to the setting sun; Pharnace, when considering the past:

> Que d'un roi qui naguère, avec quelque apparence,
> De l'aurore au couchant portait son espérance,

and Xipharès, when considering the future:

> Embrasez par nos mains le couchant et l'aurore.

As befits the great adventurer, Mithridate's natural element is the tumultuous sea, and the presence of the sea, immediate or distant, is felt throughout the play. Pharnace offers Monime the sovereignty of the sea:

> Prêts à vous recevoir, mes vaisseaux vous attendent,
> Et du pied de l'autel, vous y pouvez monter,
> Souveraine des mers qui doivent vous porter.   (I, iii)

Mithridate's sudden reappearance is signalled by the vision of his fleet on the sea:

> Princes, toute la mer est de vaisseaux couverte. (I, iv)

And Mithridate's mental picture of what a future of defeats could mean is that of a perpetual flight across the sea:

> Errant de mers en mers, et moins roi que pirate. (II, iv)

This vast world outside, the world of the conqueror and of the defeated, dramatically intrudes into the smaller, delicately poised world of the little seaport where Xipharès and Monime love each other. Therefore, the ultimate destruction of Mithridate is made particularly dramatic; the giant whose legs bestrode the ocean dies in sheltered and homely surroundings.

Not only does space shrink or expand in Racinian tragedy, but also the texture varies from one play to the next. The place chosen for the action does not always present the same amount of density and solidity. Whereas the harem in *Bajazet* stands for an unshakable spatial entity and Néron's palace suggests the power and resilience of some kind of poisonous monster, *Bérénice*, as we have seen, takes place in a stylized vacuum, between two symmetrical doors. In *Iphigénie*, although the tent of Agamemnon is the scene of the action, its value as space is negative. All our interest is directed elsewhere, towards the sea, towards distant Troy and the triumphant voyage eastwards:

> Voyez tout l'Hellespont blanchissant sous nos rames, (I, v)

and particularly towards the altar. The invisible altar is the most important place in the play, and the movements towards it or away from it compose the structural pattern of the tragedy. The distance between the tent and the altar is very short: one step in that direction for Iphigénie or Eriphile means death. The overwhelming importance of the altar comes from its ambiguous significance; it is the place where Achille and

Iphigénie will be married, and it is the place of sacrifice. This ambiguity is a source of powerful effects of dramatic irony.[1]

The choice of a rather unobtrusive and temporary setting like a tent enables Racine to stress the tension of expectancy. We are near the sea, waiting for the winds, waiting also for a sign in the sky, a miracle in nature which will reveal the final decision of the gods—in fact, for the clap of thunder Clytemnestre hears at the exact moment of the death of Eriphile:

> J'entends gronder la foudre et sens trembler la terre. (v, iv)

This enlargement of space through the suggestion of the open air is used to the full in *Phèdre*. Here there is no longer any distinction between within and without. *Phèdre* takes place before the royal palace at Trézène, and the very essence of the place is the dazzling light of the sun and the immensity of the sky. In opposition to this are the shady places forbidden to Phèdre:

> Dieux! que ne suis-je assise à l'ombre des forêts! (i, iii)

and which she imagines as the natural shelter of happy lovers:

> Dans le fond des forêts allaient-ils se cacher? (iv, vi)

or the mysterious and dark labyrinth where she dreams of re-enacting with Hippolyte the past story of Thésée and Ariane. It is also the darkness of Hell, which holds no solace for her :

> ...Fuyons dans la nuit infernale:
> Mais que dis-je? Mon père y tient l'urne fatale. (iv, vi)

Light is one of the essential themes in Phèdre, and I shall come back to it. As far as the dramatic use of space is concerned, Racine derives great advantages from the theme. While he keeps strictly to the unity of place, space in Phèdre is as vast as the sky. Here the spatial enlargement, instead of being

---

[1] One of the best analyses of Racine's use of place, directions and movements in *Iphigénie*, and particularly of the multivalency of the altar, is to be found in B. Weinberg, *The Art of Jean Racine* (Chicago, 1963), pp. 242–53.

suggested by movements (as in *Iphigénie*, towards or away from the altar), is terrifyingly static. A motionless sun, a constant merciless light confront Phèdre from the moment she appears on the stage to the moment she dies. The result is that, instead of the feeling of claustrophobia experienced in plays like *Bajazet*, we have the opposite feeling, which is as dramatically tragic, agoraphobia. The climax of this agoraphobia is reached in Act IV, scene vi, when Phèdre seeks in vain for a place where she may hide from the terrifying immensity of an inexorable sky:

> Misérable! et je vis? et je soutiens la vue
> De ce sacré Soleil dont je suis descendue?
> J'ai pour aïeul le père et le maître des Dieux;
> Le ciel, tout l'univers est plein de mes aïeux.
> Où me cacher?...

Many more illustrations could be given of the remarkable elasticity of time and place in Racine, and all within the observance of the unities. I have stressed the relevance of the playwright's various uses of these two elements. Since, in a Racinian tragedy, all patterns are interconnected, the relevance will appear even more clearly as we examine other patterns which affect time and space.

It is interesting to note that although time and space are used as conventional, ideal substances in a purely functional way, they compose a world which has a deeper kind of reality than the ordinary world where time and space are measured realistically.

This elasticity of time and space, their multivalency, implies a paradoxical quality in the situation of the Racinian hero, man; his adventures are no more than a moment, a tiny dot along the lines of time, and yet they are part of a vast historical development, and also transcend any measure of time through their very intensity. The stage where he performs his adventures is very small—a narrow prison, an empty room—and yet he participates in a vast geographical, at times cosmic, pattern.

3

THE STYLIZATION OF PASSION

Although the preceding chapter was concerned with the rule of the three unities, I left out the unity of action and I do not propose to examine it until later. Any consideration of Racine's observance of that particular convention must come after a study of the psychological elements which sustain the action in a Racinian tragedy.

It is well known that in Racine's theatre action does not depend on external events but on the feelings of the characters. The simplest illustration, and that most usually given, is taken from *Andromaque*, a play in which the whole action depends on Andromaque's feelings for Hector and Astyanax, Pyrrhus' feelings for Andromaque, Hermione's for Pyrrhus and Oreste's for Hermione. It therefore seems perfectly legitimate to use the expression 'psychological drama' to characterize Racinian tragedy. Yet the obvious is never so obvious that it cannot be denied; in any case, it must be cross-examined and qualified. This is the more necessary as various approaches to Racine have considerably complicated and obscured the issue.

Let us discard first, for the time being, the point of view of critics who study in Racine not the psychology of his characters but that of Racine himself, as revealed through his plays.[1] Our concern here is with the dramatic function of psychology, not with biographical justifications for the material used by the dramatist. We are left with a whole range of opinions on the importance of the psychological element in Racinian tragedy, but two rather extreme, and opposite, attitudes should be mentioned and, I think, dismissed.

The first is connected with the time-honoured epigram of

---

[1] This point of view will be mentioned again when I examine some aspects of Racinian criticism (see Appendix).

La Bruyère: '(Corneille) peint les hommes comme ils devraient être, (Racine) les peint tels qu'ils sont.' For many readers Racine's characters and their reactions are a poetic but faithful copy of human beings as we know them and of the kind of human behaviour which we can witness in real life. For instance, to such readers Hermione appears a most masterly and accurate study in jealousy. This is, of course, an oversimplified conception of psychological accuracy. In the twentieth century we are only too well aware of the very intricate nature of what we still call human psychology, and for many of us it implies the scientific study of the subconscious mind, complexes, etc. Therefore, some critics have endeavoured to go a step further and to test psychology in Racinian characters through more scientific, or pseudo-scientific, methods.[1] These are still based on the assumption that the reactions of Racine's characters are an exact reproduction of our own emotions.

At the other extreme, we find a point of view which seems to be gaining ground. There is a strong tendency in modern criticism towards discarding the psychological element in drama. The expression 'the psychology of characters' is almost discredited. Characters are seen more as symbols, as exponents of a particular attitude or problem, instead of being men and women of flesh and blood, with a human brain and a human heart. This approach to characterization in drama has been of great value when applied to sixteenth-century plays, or to any play where the dramatist is more interested in stylizing attitudes or symbolizing themes than in depicting the inner workings of man's sensibility. There is no doubt that a certain distrust of the psychological approach is justifiable in the case of Garnier, of the Elizabethan theatre, and perhaps of Spanish drama of the Golden Age. But this devaluation of the psychological approach has tended to spread and to affect Racinian criticism.[2]

[1] As an illustration of this method, we have the Freudian interpretation of Phèdre given by M. Turnell in *The Classical Moment* (London, 1947), p. 205.
[2] This tendency is also connected with a wish in some critics to interpret

It seems to me that both attitudes are wrong; first because the obvious is still true: Racine's tragedies are concerned with what the seventeenth century called 'l'âme humaine', that is, the mechanism of the human mind, the analysis and appreciation of man's faculties: judgment, will-power and sensibility. The whole seventeenth century, and particularly the second half, is marked by a strong interest in what, for lack of a better expression, we can still call psychological truth. Racine belongs to the same age as La Rochefoucauld, La Fontaine, Madame de La Fayette, all writers who adopted the moralist's outlook, that is, an interest in the study of man.

In considering the main features of tragedy, we saw that, while tragedy throughout the ages is characterized by a clash between man and superior forces, the nature of these terrifying forces varies with the preoccupations of a particular period. In the second half of the seventeenth century, there was a prevalent interest in the inner workings of human nature. Therefore, it was very much in keeping with the problems of the age that a dramatist should find the destructive forces threatening the tragic hero inside man himself, and that the action of tragedy should follow and illuminate the mechanism of the human mind. This is why, whereas the psychological approach to drama is on the whole anachronistic when we are dealing with sixteenth-century drama, it is on the contrary undoubtedly relevant in the case of Racine.

Secondly, the way Racine's characters feel, think, act is not a realistic copy of our psychological life. Selection and stylization intervene. This is equally true of Corneille, and the opposition between the two dramatists according to which one, Racine, is nearer to psychological reality than the other is erroneous. In both of them, we find the reality of human nature;

Racine's tragedies as the expression of man's relations with God, and for metaphysics to supersede psychology in the analysis of Racinian characters (see L. Goldmann, *Le Dieu Caché*, Paris, 1955).

in neither, a realistic transcription of it. The difference between them, on this point, is that they did not choose the same aspect of human nature as the centre of their plays.

Out of the multiple elements which compose the reality of the human condition, Racine selected a single group: the passions of love and ambition. The choice was again very closely linked with a subject which held a great fascination for his contemporaries, the passions being the most outstanding manifestations of that fundamental self-centred greed in man which the moralists found so disturbing. Some writers of the century had approached the subject either with the desire to elaborate a code of ethics intended to control such passions or with a detached intellectual curiosity towards such strange behaviour in man.[1] Racine was not concerned with an ethical purpose or with a scientific approach, but with writing tragedies, and passions in his theatre are viewed from only one angle: their potential destructive power.

Therefore 'psychology' in Racine is entirely subservient to the essential aim of tragedy: to provoke terror and pity in the audience by showing with the greatest possible intensity the full destructive effect of love and ambition. For this purpose selection is not enough. Racine's art rests on a careful stylization of passion.

The first and most obvious aspect of this stylization is the discarding of everyday life. We may note immediately that, although this discarding represents a drastic simplification of the reality we know, it conforms admirably to a deeper kind of reality. Passion is essentially an obsession which tends to push into the background all events and activities which are not directly related to itself. In Racine these are not even given a marginal importance, they are entirely absent. Only the obsession remains. In ordinary life the obsessional characteristic of

[1] For a background study of the interest displayed by the seventeenth century in man's passions, and a thorough investigation of the kind of traditions the moralists of the classical age had behind them, see A. Levi's *French Moralists, The Theory of the Passions* (Oxford, Clarendon Press), 1964.

a passion is mixed with other considerations which are part of ordinary life. Some may be relevant to our passion, some not. The components of our days make a picture which is ambiguous and approximate. We know nothing of Racinian heroes' everyday life. There is no deciphering to do as to the relevance of their day-by-day activities. There is no opportunity for Racine's characters to escape momentarily from their passion into the kind of relaxation which is the common blessing given to us all. They do not rest or sleep, or if they sleep it is in order to dream a dream which is as marked by the obsessional features of their feelings as those feelings themselves. They neither eat nor drink; or if they drink, they drink the poison which kills them. There is no suggestion of anything which, according to their personal idiosyncrasies or the pressures of their ordinary duties, could occupy their thoughts even for a few minutes, or colour their states of mind.

A most interesting case is that of Hippolyte. In previous tragedies written on the same subject, an important part of the character of Hippolyte was constituted by his daily out-of-door activities. In Seneca, in Garnier, a number of passages in the plays, and some very beautiful lines, were devoted to the themes of hunting and the taming of horses. Seneca's play starts with a long speech by Hippolyte in which the young man gives precise technical orders to his fellow hunters. Garnier's Hippolyte is constantly seen against his background of forest, and he seems to carry with him the smell of bracken and wild animals. Racine has sacrificed what in Garnier was ever-present in the foreground.

Hippolyte's interest in horses and hunting are mentioned, but negatively, first by Théramène:

> On vous voit moins souvent, orgueilleux et sauvage,
> Tantôt faire voler un char sur le rivage,
> Tantôt, savant dans l'art par Neptune inventé,
> Rendre docile au frein un coursier indompté.   (I, i)

and then by Hippolyte himself:

> Mon arc, mes javelots, mon char, tout m'importune;
> Je ne me souviens plus des leçons de Neptune;
> Mes seuls gémissements font retentir les bois,
> Et mes coursiers oisifs ont oublié ma voix. (II, ii)

These two passages are not intended as a way of building up the character of Hippolyte. It is very clear that hunting is no longer part of himself. The mention of those past activities has a precise dramatic function: the passages I have quoted are both closely connected with the death of Hippolyte and are meant to increase the tragic impact of this death, by an effect of dramatic irony. Neptune is seen by Théramène as a friend of the young man, by Hippolyte as a half-forgotten friend; and at the end of the play will prove his enemy. We also perceive the final irony in the reversal of situation during the battle with the monster: the successful hunter is hunted by the beast. And the most cruel touch or irony is that a man who could 'rendre docile un coursier indompté' should be trampled to death by his own horses 'que sa main a nourris'; this effect of irony being moreover felt by the audience, long before the end, in the unconscious foreboding of the hero:

> Et mes coursiers oisifs ont oublié ma voix.

The discarding of all the impure elements of everyday life is made easier by the unity of place. In the 'ideal' place where the tragedy unfolds, the characters are altogether cut off from all the other places which would be the normal setting for their day-by-day activities.

Not only are passions thus disentangled from the criss-cross texture of actual life, but they are also presented in such a way that the whole attention of the audience is necessarily focused on them, to the exclusion of everything else.

It is a remarkable feature of Racinian tragedy that the playwright does not try to achieve dramatic suspense by provoking the curiosity of the spectators as regards the events which will take place during the play. All his plots are well-known stories. We know beforehand that Britannicus will be murdered by Néron, Athalie defeated by God, Hippolyte killed by the monster from the sea. Even the story of Bajazet was known to the public when Racine wrote the play. Whenever Racine alters slightly the traditional plot, as, for instance, in *Iphigénie* by introducing Eriphile, who in the end will be the victim intended by the gods, he is very careful to destroy every possible effect of surprise which we might have at the end, when Eriphile's fate is revealed. Throughout the play we are given a number of hints which enable us to guess, easily and by degrees, what is bound to happen. The situation of Aricie in *Phèdre* is made very clear from the beginning, including her love for Hippolyte and his for her.[1]

Does this mean, then, that there is no surprise, no dramatic suspense, in Racine? No; the guessing, the wondering, the suspense thus removed from the audience are the share of the characters, and these we experience vicariously through them.

With a foreknowledge of Titus' and Bérénice's future separation (*invitus invitam dimisit*), we witness her ill-founded sense of security:

> Le temps n'est plus, Phénice, où je pouvais trembler.   (I, v)

her anxious efforts to interpret Titus' attitude:

> Qu'ai-je fait? Que veut-il? Et que dit ce silence?
> . . . . . .
> Je ne respire pas dans cette incertitude.   (II, v)

and her mistaken surmise,

> L'amour d'Antiochus l'a peut-être offensé.
> . . . . . .
> Si Titus est jaloux, Titus est amoureux.   (II, v)

---

[1] This aspect of Racine's dramatic technique has been studied in detail, most illuminatingly, by G. May in 'Tragédie cornélienne, tragédie racinienne', in *Illinois Studies in Language and Literature*, vol. XXXII, ch. III.

We are not surprised when Thésée returns to Athens. We have been well prepared for this event, but Phèdre has not, and it is *her* horrified shock which accounts for the dramatic impact of Œnone's words:

> Il faut d'un vain amour étouffer la pensée,
> Madame. Rappelez votre vertu passée.
> Le Roi, qu'on a cru mort, va paraître à vos yeux;
> Thésée est arrivé, Thésée est en ces lieux.　　　(III, iii)

Thanks to this deliberate focusing of the dramatic suspense on the characters themselves, we, the audience, having no personal curiosity as to the successive events in the play and the final outcome, concentrate entirely on the reactions of the characters to these events.

Here again, surprise is not the effect wanted by the dramatist. To begin with, the passions which are going to work within each character are clearly revealed to us at the beginning of the play. As I suggested in the preceding chapter, we never see the beginning nor the end of a sentiment in the Racinian theatre; therefore any kind of interest which could be produced by the sudden emergence of a feeling of love or hatred, by an unexpected volte-face in a character's attitude, is entirely discarded.

Passion, once given, follows a rigorously logical mechanism, and every reaction of the characters strikes us with a forceful impression of its inevitability.

When Phèdre discovers Hippolyte's love for Aricie (which is no discovery for the audience), she discovers also terrifying reactions in herself caused by the violence of her jealousy:

> Il faut perdre Aricie. Il faut de mon époux
> Contre un sang odieux réveiller le courroux.
> Qu'il ne se borne pas à des peines légères:
> Le crime de la sœur passe celui des frères.
> Dans mes jaloux transports je le veux implorer.
> Que fais-je? Où ma raison se va-t'elle égarer?
> 　　　　　　　　　　　　　　　　　　(IV, vi)

The spectators watch her going through the harrowing process of self-discovery, while well aware themselves that her criminal thoughts, the frenzied disorder of her mind, the increased feeling of guilt are all part of the logical working of her passion.

It is the relentless logic of the mechanism of passion which produces an intense emotion of terror in the audience. Every shade of feeling in a character is, if not foreseen, at least immediately acknowledged by us as the rational and inevitable consequence of what precedes. The superior forces which destroy the tragic heroes wear no masks as far as we are concerned, nor is their strategy baffling. Hence an agonizing feeling of helplessness in us, born of the kind of endorsement our reason gives to what our sensibility would reject.

But the mechanism of passion can only work with such implacable and impeccable precision because of certain premisses which are taken for granted and represent another aspect of stylization. Different in this respect from our world, the Racinian theatre is a world of absolute values. The hero commits himself completely to his passion: Oreste's love for Hermione, Phèdre's for Hippolyte, are absolute values. The clash inside a character is always between two feelings which admit of nothing else but their own existence, and this gives to any dilemma a particular tragic intensity. Andromaque's love for Hector and her love for her son are equally absolute, and the only values. Logically there is no solution for her. In *Bajazet* Atalide is torn between two feelings which have the same quality of absoluteness: Bajazet's life and Bajazet's love; and no other element can interfere and modify the balance of forces inside her. Titus' position is that of a total commitment to Rome:

> Ma gloire inexorable à toute heure me suit; (VI, vi)

and a total commitment to Bérénice:

> Tout ce que j'aimerai jusqu'au dernier soupir. (III, i)

Any form of compromise is impossible. Andromaque's plan: to marry Pyrrhus to save her son, and then kill herself to remain faithful to Hector, will never be carried out; it is a pitiful illusion of a possible escape from the laws which govern the Racinian universe. So is Titus' desperate move near the end of the play, when he contemplates suicide; by doing so he would go against the dictates of the two absolute values which rule his life.

Absolute passion cannot lessen in any degree its intensity nor make room for considerations of lesser importance. Therefore Bajazet cannot, even to save his life, give Roxane the smallest share of his heart. And Hermione's expression of kindness to Oreste,

> Vous que j'ai plaint, enfin que je voudrais aimer.   (II, ii)

is rightly dismissed by Oreste as an insulting pretence:

> Je vous entends. Tel est mon partage funeste:
> Le cœur est pour Pyrrhus, et les vœux pour Oreste.   (II, ii)

There is no possibility whatever, in the Racinian tragedy, that the feelings of the characters, or their set of values, can be altered; and, accordingly, the destructive mechanism of passion will work in its inexorable way, free from that dust of secondary considerations which so often in real life clogs the movement of our strongest feelings. For if, in ordinary life, passions have also at times this characteristic of absolute value, the mechanism according to which they work does not necessarily follow the perfect logic which leads to destruction. Other things intervene, and particularly the irrational elements, such as sudden impulses coming from deeper within, and, most important of all, the time element. Time brings with it a succession of ever-changing moods, time offers moments of relaxation in the middle of the most intense experience of passion, time wears away passion and accounts for such states of mind as indifference and resignation.

This is where the particular nature of conventional time is

exploited to the full by Racine: the feelings of his characters are entirely free from the effects of duration. Passion is always at the same pitch of intensity.

Resignation holds no meaning when present and future, reality and illusion, are one single passionate move forward. Even after the death of Pyrrhus, Hermione refuses to act, think, or feel differently:

> Il m'aimerait peut-être. Il le feindrait du moins.   (v, iii)

Racinian heroes experience defeat and destruction. After her terrible dry 'Dieu des Juifs, tu l'emportes', Athalie's feelings are unchanged. Titus, Bérénice and Antiochus accept separation, but there is no hint of resignation in their final parting. In this case, paradoxically, their timeless feelings are carried over into endless duration, the three characters eternally tortured by the despair of absence:

> Que le jour recommence et que le jour finisse,
> Sans que jamais Titus puisse voir Bérénice,
> Sans que de tout le jour je puisse voir Titus!   (iv, v)

Racine's handling of the time factor in the course of the play increases also the relentless characteristic of the mechanism of passion, by never allowing his characters any moments of re- laxation between the scenes. The wheels never stop running, without a pause, without a break, and with the same lethal efficiency, whether a character is on the stage or off. To this impression the conventions of time and place contribute greatly, as well as the discarding of everyday life; and the advantages of such conventions are skilfully used by Racine in the careful way he links the different scenes together. The entrance or exit of a character is not only fully justified, but its motivation is part of the mechanism.[1] Any hint of a character being on the

---

[1] Many Racinian critics have commented on Racine's careful craftsmanship in the linking of scenes. See J. Scherer, *La dramaturgie classique en France* (Paris, 1950), and particularly Professor Lapp's analyses in *Aspects of Racinian Tragedy*, pp. 114–20.

point of doing something off-stage or of having just done it is so closely related to what is taking place on the stage as to be part of the same atmosphere, the same moment, the same revolution of the wheel.

So it is with the visit to Pallas, in *Britannicus*, which at the end of Act I motivates Agrippine's exits (scene iii):

> (*to Britannicus*)...
> Je ne m'explique point. Si vous voulez m'entendre,
> Suivez-moi chez Pallas, où je vais vous attendre;

and that of Britannicus, shortly afterwards (scene iv):

> (*to Narcisse*)...
> Surtout dans ce palais remarque avec adresse
> Avec quel soin Néron fait garder la Princesse.
> ......
> Cependant de Néron je vais trouver la mère
> Chez Pallas, comme toi l'affranchi de mon père.
> Je vais la voir, l'aigrir, la suivre, et s'il se peut,
> M'engager sous son nom plus loin qu'elle ne veut.

This is the end of Act I: and Act II shows us almost immediately Narcisse coming to Néron, as if to carry out Britannicus' injunction.

The visit to Pallas is mentioned by Néron as a possibility:

> Pallas de ses conseils empoisonne ma mère;
> Il séduit chaque jour Britannicus mon frère.
> Ils l'écoutent tout seul; et qui suivrait leurs pas
> Les trouverait peut-être assemblés chez Pallas.   (II, i)

This possibility is at once confirmed by Narcisse:

> Vos ennemis, déchus de leur vaine espérance,
> Sont allés chez Pallas pleurer leur impuissance.   (II, ii)

The off-stage meeting in Pallas' house is thus made part of Agrippine's illusions on her political acumen, Britannicus' impatient wish to fight, Néron's growing irritation, and Narcisse's treacherous delight.

The stress is therefore on the present significance of the meeting as part of the general movement of the different passions which actuate the plot. Moreover, the place of the meeting, Pallas' house, partakes of the same atmosphere of underhand scheming and plotting as the palace itself, so that it appears to make one with it.

But, as a rule, we are not conscious of characters being elsewhere. They seem always there, ever ready to appear, either to obey or to contradict a wish expressed by a character who is actually speaking. Thus Bajazet asserts his presence beside Atalide at the very moment when she has decided to avoid meeting him:

> Mais non, je lui veux bien épargner ce souci:
> Il ne me verra plus.
> ZAÏRE   Madame, le voici.   (III, iii)

and at the end of the following scene Bajazet's determination to undeceive Roxane seems to provoke her entrance:

> Roxane n'est pas loin; laissez agir ma foi.
> J'irai, bien plus content et de vous et de moi,
> Détromper son amour d'une feinte forcée,
> Que je n'allais tantôt déguiser ma pensée.
> La voici.   (III, iv)

'Roxane n'est pas loin' has the value of an understatement. We knew she could not be elsewhere and had not stopped circling round Bajazet, unceasingly on the alert, ready to spring.

The impression of strain, of some invisible chain pulling the characters towards one another, is constant throughout Racinian tragedy. This is the kind of tension we find in Pyrrhus' obsession with Andromaque. When he interrupts a conversation with his confidant to welcome Andromaque:

> Une autre fois je t'ouvrirai mon âme:
> Andromaque paraît.   (I, iii)

Andromaque seems not to have entered the room, but to have been conjured up from within the very heart of Pyrrhus. When he has decided to give her up, the same obsession directs his movements towards her:

> Retournons-y. Je veux la braver à sa vue.　　　(II, v)

In Act III the same movement takes on more urgency and impatience—

> Où donc est la Princesse?　　　(III, vi)

and reaches a desperate urge in his fierce attempts to win Andromaque:

> Songez-y: je vous laisse; et je viendrai vous prendre
> Pour vous mener au temple, où ce fils doit m'attendre;
> Et là vous me verrez, soumis ou furieux,
> Vous couronner, Madame, ou le perdre à vos yeux.　　(III, vii)

From then on he is carried forward by this movement towards the expected goal of all his efforts. In Act IV Hermione realizes bitterly that, while she is talking, his whole being is irresistibly dragged elsewhere, towards Andromaque:

> Tu lui parles du cœur, tu la cherches des yeux.　　(IV, v)

and our final vision of Pyrrhus at the end of Act IV, when he leaves his confidant, is that of a man almost in a trance, yielding to some kind of magnetic pull, tense and triumphant, and deaf to Phœnix' warning:

> Andromaque m'attend. Phœnix, garde son fils.　　(IV, vi)

The effect of tension in the uninterrupted movement which leads the hero to the final catastrophe is inseparable from another aspect of the stylization of passion: in the Racinian universe, passion is always frustrated. It is of course a well-known psychological truth that frustration can make passion dangerous. Racine has used this possibility to the full. None of his heroes is ever allowed the satisfaction of coming one step nearer the fulfilment of his love or ambition.

Between these passionate lovers, no act of love will ever take place, nor has any ever occurred. Racine makes it clear that

Bérénice was not Titus' mistress. In the preface to *Andromaque* he explains that he has not followed Euripides in making Andromaque Pyrrhus' concubine. He says, 'Et je doute que les larmes d'Andromaque eussent fait sur l'esprit de mes spectateurs l'impression qu'elles ont faite, si elles avaient coulé pour un autre fils que celui qu'elle avait d'Hector.' One of the reasons for this departure from Euripides is to keep Andromaque's love for Hector as an absolute value. The other is to create in Pyrrhus a state of complete frustration which destroys him. The convention of the *bienséances* proves most useful in achieving this particular purpose: there can be no possible ambiguity in the relations between the characters; the fulfilment of love can be achieved only through marriage. That simple and economical convention has been used by Racine to its maximum scope. Mutual love in his tragedies is as frustrated as unrequited love. An interesting case of the tragic value of the convention of marriage is that of Aricie's refusal to go away with Hippolyte unless they are married. Some critics have been rather scornful of her attitude, and have referred to her as a 'demoiselle de pensionnat' motivated by bourgeois scruples. That, to my mind, is a misunderstanding of the point. If Aricie had agreed to escape with Hippolyte without either of them mentioning marriage (contrary to the convention), it would have suggested to the audience, if not an immediate physical fulfilment of their love, at least some kind of closer intimacy. It is essential, to underline their tragic destiny, that Hippolyte and Aricie should never reach together, both alive, the temple outside the gates of the city where they have planned to exchange their solemn vows. Fulfilment must be, without any ambiguity, beyond reach.

Ambition is frustrated in the same way as love, producing the same strain, the same desperate tension in the character. The awareness of defeat—'Ma place est occupée et je ne suis plus rien', says Agrippine (Act III, scene iv) and 'Je suis vaincu', states

Mithridate (II, iii)—acts as an incentive and provokes the hero to more feverish scheming, more ambitious dreams of conquest. It is perhaps in Agrippine that this impression of restless activity, the more dangerous for being kept in check by circumstances, may be seen most clearly. The restlessness is apparent from the very first scene, when her confidant finds her prowling unescorted in the palace, trying to discover Néron's secrets, in the humiliating position of waiting behind a locked door and yet fiercely determined. The pressure of the pent-up feelings, the raging bitterness of being constantly baulked in all her manœuvres, is such that it almost reaches bursting point in her discussion with Burrhus:

> Ah! l'on s'efforce en vain de me fermer la bouche,   (III, iii)

when she threatens to make public all the crimes which have led Néron to power:

> Je confesserai tout, exil, assassinats,
> Poison même......   (III, iii)

to be, once more, checked by Burrhus' cold remark:

> Madame, ils ne vous croiront pas.   (III, iii)

And it is the presence in Agrippine's mind of those seething impulses, so painfully contained, which creates the almost unbearable tension in her conversation with Néron in Act IV.

The effect of frustration is emphasized by the absence of any physical action on the stage. The stage conventions require perfect decorum. Characters can never release even their strongest emotions by a single gesture which would carry with it the violence of their feelings. An invisible wall between the protagonists does not allow the slightest physical contact. Néron cannot seize Junie's hand, Mithridate cannot strike his treacherous son. Words alone can provide an outlet for the frustrated passion. And here the decorum of language increases still further the dramatic effect of strain.

★

I have so far considered the Racinian characters singly. Stylization is found also in the relations which Racine establishes between them, and which are such that they complicate and intensify the terrifying workings of love and ambition. For not only is man destroyed by his own passions, but also he destroys others. Oreste does not only destroy himself, but destroys Pyrrhus as well. Racine places his characters according to a stylized pattern of relations which enables the destructive forces of passion to operate with the greatest possible effect.

It has been said that the subjects of Racine's tragedies were as banal, as realistic, as the crime stories we read in newspapers. Nothing is further from the truth. His subjects are, on the contrary, extraordinary, although well known. Tradition had provided the stylized patterns; past tragic dramatists had already extracted from the criminal records of mankind the quintessence of the most horrible situations. Some of those situations were selected by Racine as particularly suitable for his purpose, and he made full use of their explosive potentialities.

The best way to ensure that dangerous human beings should harm each other is to bring them together as closely as possible. The closest links of all are probably family ties. They are natural bonds, universally acknowledged and held sacred, and therefore the disruption in family relations caused by passion will appear more tragic.

The violation of the natural order is immediately apparent in some situations verging on the monstrous or the incredible. In *Iphigénie* a father is to murder his own daughter; in *Mithridate* a man and his two sons are in love with the same woman. But the tragedy inherent in such subjects depends very much on our awareness of intimacy, as well as of estrangement, in family relations. In that respect one might be tempted to say that *Iphigénie* and *Britannicus* are more successful than *Mithridate*. There is little in the latter play which suggests close relations between Mithridate and his sons, or between the two brothers. Xipharès' attitude towards his father is composed of dutiful respect and the sense that he must atone for his mother's past treason. Pharnace appears fundamentally as a stranger to Mithridate and his brother. Mithridate himself is presented as a man without much paternal feeling:

> Et nous l'avons vu même à ses cruels soupçons
> Sacrifier deux fils pour de moindres raisons. (I, v)

Even when he hesitates to kill Xipharès, his wish to spare him is mainly dictated by considerations of expediency:

> Tu vas sacrifier, qui? malheureux! Ton fils!
> Un fils que Rome craint? qui peut venger son père?
> Pourquoi répandre un sang qui m'est si nécessaire? (IV, v)

Undoubtedly this stress on unnatural reactions carries with it its particular tragic effects, for it emphasizes the warped outlook of desperate ambition. His passion for domination has long since established between him and his sons the kind of relationship in which he expects only obedience from them, and they can only have towards him reactions of admiration, respect, fear or loathing. Hence the rather impersonal way in which the two brothers refer to Mithridate, calling him 'le roi' more often than 'mon père'. This icy atmosphere surrounding family relations, this deliberate distance between father and sons is in keeping with the pattern of the play, where attitudes of cold dignity are constantly opposed to the fiery outbursts of Mithridate.

On the contrary, closeness of relations is stressed throughout *Iphigénie*. In Agamemnon all the natural reactions of paternal love are strongly emphasized, as well as the mutual love between father and daughter—and that from the very beginning of the play:

Ma fille...Ce nom seul, dont les droits sont si saints,
Sa jeunesse, mon sang, n'est pas ce que je plains.
Je plains mille vertus, une amour mutuelle,
Sa piété pour moi, ma tendresse pour elle,...   (I, i)

The words 'mère', 'fille', 'père' recur constantly. Even the absent brother of Iphigénie, Oreste, is mentioned in that first scene:

Votre Oreste au berceau va-t-il finir sa vie?

The very strong awareness the three characters in the play—Agamemnon, Iphigénie and Clytemnestre—have of their relationships as parents and child, husband and wife, put them in a unique position to be hurt and to hurt. They may hurt unconsciously, as Iphigénie does in her innocent remark to her father:

Verra-t-on à l'autel votre heureuse famille?   (II, ii)

Most of the time, however, the characters are only too well aware of their power to hurt. The tragic element in the relationship between Agamemnon and Clytemnestre is intensified by the intimate knowledge they have of each other. Agamemnon realizes that only cunning, and that of doubtful efficacy, can be his defensive weapon against a woman whose flashing intuitions and potential violence are well known to him. Clytemnestre's insight into her husband's heart gives her terrifying possibilities which she exploits fully in the quarrel scene of Act IV, when she directs her thrusts, with exquisite accuracy, to the most vulnerable places.

The same dangerous closeness marks the very complex relationships between Agrippine and Néron. Here again family ties assume particular and disturbing features. The natural influence a mother has over her son results in the almost pathological uneasiness Néron feels in the presence of Agrippine. With her the normal pride in finding family resemblances in one's children becomes the horrified realization of Néron's hereditary taints:

Des fiers Domitius l'humeur triste et sauvage.   (I, i)

49

All the alarming aspects of this particular relationship come into play in the great scene of Act IV. There the complexity of Néron's and Agrippine's attitudes towards each other is such as to give several layers of meaning to every statement they make:[1] to the basic ambiguity of two partners in crime who are also two enemies frightened of each other is added the ambiguous position of a mother and her son constantly reminding each other of this intimate tie and using it as one more weapon for attack or defence. The tragic import of this desperate duel is ironically underlined by the concluding words of the scene, spoken by Néron, which deceptively stress the importance of family relations:

> Allez donc, et portez cette joie à mon frère.
> Gardes, qu'on obéisse aux ordres de ma mère.   (IV, ii)

Closeness of relations can be ensured in other ways, and is in Racine very much connected with his use of the unity of place. Prison is a sure means of keeping human beings together. Andromaque and Astyanax are the prisoners of Pyrrhus, Aricie of Thésée, Junie of Néron. This not only brings the characters together, it creates a very dangerous relation, as it enables one human being to be master of the life of another. The relation of the gaoler and the prisoner colours all the conversations between Pyrrhus and Andromaque. The same relation enables Néron to watch closely and torture Junie and Britannicus. In *Bajazet* the gaoler–prisoner situation becomes that of master and slave. Roxane, a slave herself, but with power of life and death over Bajazet, pursues relentlessly her passionate and ultimate purpose of enslaving his heart. In her mind love is identified with this abominable relation of master and slave, and this identification comes out in such statements as these:

---

[1] The ambiguity of this scene has been analysed convincingly, if somewhat crudely and incompletely, by René-Albert Gutman in his book *Introduction à la Lecture des Poètes français* (Paris, 1946).

Songez-vous que je tiens les portes du Palais,
Que je puis vous l'ouvrir ou fermer pour jamais,
Que j'ai sur votre vie un empire suprême,
Que vous ne respirez qu'autant que je vous aime?
Et sans ce même amour, qu'offensent vos refus,
Songez-vous, en un mot, que vous ne seriez plus?   (ii, i)

Bajazet is thus less than a slave. He is merely an emanation of Roxane's will. His very breathing is entirely dependent on her and his precarious existence can, at any minute, be turned not so much into a corpse as into nothingness.

★

It is therefore in this tightly woven network of relations that the logical working of passion will function. The passions of love and ambition are self-centred, and in Racine the stylization of passion implies total self-centredness. As a result, whatever the closeness between the characters, one aspect of human relationships is entirely absent: human sympathy. It is impossible for a Racinian character to detach his thoughts or feeling from the problem of his passion. If he takes into consideration, or is moved by, the feelings of another character, it is only in so far as they affect his own situation. Accordingly pity and tenderness are emotions for which there is no room, no time, no relevance in the Racinian universe. The absence of such emotions increases considerably the tragic intensity. A moment of pity for the man or woman one hurts would mean a moment of respite, an effort to counteract the brutal consequences of misfortune, an accidental disturbance which might put the working of the tragedy out of gear. A moment of tenderness is a moment of comparative peace, which relaxes the tension and is therefore incompatible with the relentless uniformity of intense feelings.

On very rare occasions the possibility of being moved by a feeling of pity is mentioned by a Racinian hero, but only when it is a dangerous impulse which, far from relaxing the tragic tension, brings the hero nearer to destruction. Athalie is quite rightly frightened by her reaction in the presence of the child

Joas:

> Quel prodige nouveau me trouble et m'embarrasse?
> La douceur de sa voix, son enfance, sa grâce,
> Font insensiblement à mon inimitié
> Succéder... Je serais sensible à la pitié? (II, vii)

The feeling is alien, unaccountable; Athalie is aware of it as a kind of terrifying aberration. It is in fact the most unfair trap laid by God for her downfall.

Or else the expression of pity is no more than a condescending gesture, a hypocritical statement destined to retain for a time a lover who might be useful, as when Hermione says to Oreste:

> Vous que j'ai plaint, enfin que je voudrais aimer. (II, ii)

It is in vain that at times one character appeals to the better feelings of another. Andromaque's efforts to move Hermione in favour of her son are rejected with ironical cruelty:

> S'il faut fléchir Pyrrhus, qui le peut mieux que vous?
>
> (III, iv)

Junie's first impulse to stop Néron from arresting Britannicus:

> Que faites-vous?
> C'est votre frère... (III, viii)

is soon checked by her own realization that any plea is useless:

> ...Hélas! C'est un amant jaloux. (III, viii)

Mithridate tries in vain to make Monime sympathize with his present situation as a defeated warrior, even suggesting that it would be a noble part to play, if she were to stay loyally by the side of a lonely man persecuted by fate:

> N'était-il pas plus noble, et plus digne de vous,
> ......
> D'opposer votre estime au destin qui m'outrage,
> Et de me rassurer, en flattant ma douleur,
> Contre la défiance attachée au malheur?

Monime's answer, cold, dignified and disdainful—

> J'obéis. N'est-ce pas assez me faire entendre? (II, iv)

—shows that she is unmoved by this attempt to attract her sympathy.

It would indeed be wrong to think that this incapacity in a Racinian character to put himself for one second in the place of someone else and thus experience human sympathy exists only in fierce characters like Néron or Roxane. It is a characteristic of all Racinian heroes, even those who might appear endowed with a gentler sensibility. Bérénice does not pity Antiochus, or Antiochus Bérénice, and this gives a particular flavour of desperate harshness to all their dialogues. The long speech in which he tells her of his love and sufferings is dismissed by Bérénice as an ill-timed declaration:

> Seigneur, je n'ai pas cru que dans une journée
> Qui doit avec César unir ma destinée,
> Il fût quelque mortel qui pût impunément
> Se venir à mes yeux déclarer mon amant. (I, iv)

This complete lack of sympathy and understanding is matched by the same self-centred reaction of Antiochus when he gives Bérénice the terrible message from Titus. Not for one second does he stop to consider Bérénice's suffering; his only concern is for the advancement of his own suit and the only emotion he feels is indignation and self-pity when Bérénice dismisses him from her presence without even looking at him:

> Ne me trompé-je point? L'ai-je bien entendue?
> Que je me garde, moi, de paraître à sa vue?
> . . . . . .
> Moi, je demeurerai pour me voir dédaigner? (IV, iii)

Tenderness might be expected in family relations, especially when they are very close, as in *Iphigénie*, and indeed Agamemnon recalls with shame his daughter's 'piété pour moi'. But here again tenderness is pushed aside, to leave only the violence of egocentric passions.

Agamemnon's and Clytemnestre's love for their daugher is a passionate extension of self-love. In their terrible quarrel, which takes place in her presence, they seem unaware of what she may feel, and are only concerned with their own sufferings:

AGAMEMNON Allez; et que les Grecs, qui vont vous immoler,
Reconnaissent *mon* sang en le voyant couler. (IV, iv)

The horror of the planned sacrifice is experienced by Clytemnestre as it affects herself, not her daughter; she also mentions

...du plus pur de *mon* sang,   (IV, iv)

and conjures up with harrowing vividness the contrast between her arrival with Iphigénie and the grim and lonely return:

Et *moi*, qui l'amenai triomphante, adorée,
Je m'en retournerai seule et désespérée?
Je verrai les chemins encor tout parfumés
Des fleurs dont sous ses pas on les avait semés? (IV, iv)

Even Iphigénie does not display the emotion of tenderness which one would have expected from her past behaviour towards her father. The cold tone of her speech to Agamemnon shows how far she is from any form of *attendrissement*:

Mon père,
Cessez de vous troubler, vous n'êtes point trahi.
Quand vous commanderez, vous serez obéi.
Ma vie est votre bien...   (IV, iv)

On the other hand, she expresses some tender concern for her parents when she takes leave of her mother. But tenderness here is a particularly effective form of tragic irony:

Ne reprochez jamais mon trépas à mon père.
......
Vos yeux me reverront dans Oreste mon frère.
Puisse-t-il être, hélas! moins funeste à sa mère! (V, iii)

The loving words of comfort and blessing conjure up the hideous vision of Clytemnestre's future crime and of her murder. In a world in which pity and tenderness are either absent, or else a sinister mockery of sympathy, cruelty will appear in all its glaring brutality. Everything which stands in the way of passion must be destroyed: 'Il faut perdre Aricie,' says Phèdre (IV, vi). Every means of achieving the satisfaction of passion must be tried; even the ruthless blackmail Pyrrhus uses against Andromaque:

> Vous couronner, Madame, ou le perdre à vos yeux.
>
> (III, vii)

As a supreme test of Bajazet's loyalty to her, Roxane proposes to have Atalide killed before his eyes:

> Ma rivale est ici. Suis-moi sans différer.
> Dans les mains des muets viens la voir expirer.   (V, iv)

Both Hermione and Oreste are Pyrrhus' murderers, each led by the destructive nature of passion.

Moreover, an atmosphere of cruelty suffuses most of the Racinian tragedies. In *Athalie*, the recurrent use of the word 'sang', the images of wild animals, the relation of past slaughters, compose a fitting background for Mathan's cynical cruelty:

> Qu'importe qu'au hasard un sang vil soit versé?   (II, v)

or Joad's fierce injunctions to his Levites:

> Dans l'infidèle sang baignez-vous sans horreur.
> Frappez et Tyriens, et même Israélites.
> Ne descendez-vous pas de ces fameux lévites
> Qui lorsqu'au Dieu du Nil le volage Israël
> Rendit dans le désert un culte criminel,
> De leurs plus chers parents saintement homicides,
> Consacrèrent leurs mains dans le sang des perfides. (IV, iii)

A casual remark indicates how little value a human life has in the cruel world of Néron's court:

> NARCISSE   ...La fameuse Locuste
> A redoublé pour moi ses soins officieux:
> Elle a fait expirer un esclave à mes yeux.   (IV, iv)

References to the past and future cruelty of the heroes help to emphasize still further the destructive ferocity. Athalie's past crimes, Pyrrhus' bloody deeds in the Trojan war, Mithridate's previous murder of two sons, are as much part of the character's personality as are Néron's future matricide and Clytemnestre's future crime.

Even more alarming perhaps is the part played by unconscious cruelty. That, also, inevitably results from the impeccable working of stylized passion. The Racinian character, although very conscious of the effect his words can have, is aware of their effect only in connection with the self-centred purpose inspired by his own passion; he cannot foresee the reactions caused by feelings irrelevant to his own obsession.

In Act IV, scene v, of *Andromaque*, Pyrrhus, stung by Hermione's ironical reminder of the part he played in the downfall of Troy, interprets Hermione's bitter sarcasm as a reaction of hurt pride and assumes as a retort a cool and dignified attitude. It is in fact extremely convenient for him to see in Hermione's scornful irony a proof of indifference towards him. The real feelings of Hermione are something which in themselves have never attracted his notice. And he does not realize the unbearable cruelty of his words:

> J'ai craint de vous trahir, peut-être je vous sers.
> Nos cœurs n'étaient point faits dépendants l'un de l'autre;
> Je suivais mon devoir, et vous cédiez au vôtre.
> Rien ne vous engageait à m'aimer en effet.

Shut within the complex and yet narrow circle of his passion, the Racinian character is completely blind to all the rest. This is why even the characters who appear most harmless can inflict the most refined tortures on others. And Iphigénie is perhaps of all the Racinian heroines the one whose most well-meaning remarks convey the cruellest intimations.

4

THE PARADOX OF THE 'HÉROS MOYEN'

It is not enough to watch with horrified fascination the torturing effects and catastrophic results of a relentless mechanism. Terror is only one side of the tragic emotion experienced by the spectators. It is essential that they should sympathize with the characters, feel pity for them, and that terror should not be prompted only by the intellectual grasp of the general pattern but be felt immediately and through our sensibility. Therefore the characters must not be symbolic figures endowed with the clockwork precision we expect from a mathematical pattern, but creatures of flesh and blood. This Racine achieves with the greatest economy as, in his theatre, the same features which contribute to the terrifying effect of the tragic mechanism are also directed towards the illusion the audience has of watching real men and women.

★

The first reason why Racinian characters appear to us so lifelike, so close to ourselves, is that we understand them perfectly. In order to provide this perfect understanding, Racine has used both the simplifying process of selection and a technique involving extreme complexity.

The seventeenth-century interest in what is most basic and most general in man resulted in selecting what could be easily understood by the public. Racine, like the other classicists, presents passions in the most characteristic form they assume in the human condition: love of a man for a woman, of a woman for a man, and ambition in its most widely acknowledged form, greed for political power. This is an elementary and obvious point, but it must be made. Passion presented thus is more immediately and more completely intelligible to an audience than passion taking the form of particular idiosyncrasies such as Cousin Pons's love for his collection of pictures, or, in the modern novel *Lolita*, the hero's fatal obsession with nymphets, although such passions are equally destructive.

It is, I think, in the light of this choice, common to all the classicists, that we should interpret the concept of the Racinian *héros moyen*. The passage in the preface to *Andromaque*, in which Racine, following Aristotle, states that tragic heroes must be 'ni tout à fait bons, ni tout à fait méchants' is well known. But it has caused a number of misconceptions. It has led some people to think that Racinian characters, having 'une bonté médiocre', represent an average type of humanity and as such should attract the sympathy of the spectator by the similarity they present to the people he meets in ordinary life, and to himself.

In fact, it is evident that, even without mentioning their positions as kings and queens, princes and princesses, Racine's characters, because of the stylization of their passions (timelessness, absolute values, etc.) are very different from the spectator. Nor are they representative of an average morality. Some, like Néron or Roxane, are patently worse than average humanity and some, like Junie or Titus, better and nobler. The moral significance of the Racinian tragedy raises problems which will be discussed later, but moral judgments on the characters do not help to clarify the concept of the *héros moyen*.

On the other hand, once we have discarded the assumption that the *héros moyen* implies a copy of the man in the street, it is easier to see the kind of selection and of stylization which is found here. The selection bears, not on the type of hero chosen, but on the range of feelings and thoughts he expresses, which are all within the scope of the experience and imagination of the audience. Pity and sympathy depend not so much on the moral judgment passed on the hero as on the possibility of understanding him. The best illustration of Racine's concern for keeping the reactions of a character within the grasp of the audience is to be found in his handling of Néron. The dramatist makes it clear in his two prefaces that he never thought of Néron in any other way than as an evil personality and he even defends himself against the charge of having softened the portrait. But Néron as a fully fledged monster would be beyond normal human experience. The play is centred on a Néron who is evil but humanly understandable, and the tragedy stops at the point where he becomes separated from the audience by the opacity of the monster's idiosyncrasies.

A close understanding of the characters' feelings is an essential part of Racinian tragedy. The knowledge which the audience possesses of the hero's states of mind is complete and unbroken. This is of course required by the form the destructive forces of tragedy take in Racine: in order to perceive the logical working of passions, it is necessary to perceive every single move dictated by them, and every link between one move and the next. But at the same time this perfect knowledge is imparted in such a way that it creates between the characters and the audience a kind of intimacy which goes far beyond the intellectual requirement.

Racine's characters are endowed with a gift for self-revelation which illuminates every nuance of their feelings. Self-revelation should not be confused with self-analysis, which implies a detached attitude while scrutinizing oneself, and a certain objectivity in the probing. There is nothing of the kind in the Racinian hero. The illuminating searchlight is guided by passion alone, for its own purposes, and the constant shifts in direction follow the restless moves of the character's sensibility.

A few examples will show the effect produced on the spectator by this illumination.

HERMIONE   Hélas! pour mon malheur, je l'ai trop écouté.
　　　　　　Je n'ai point du silence affecté le mystère:
　　　　　　Je croyais sans péril pouvoir être sincère;

Et sans armer mes yeux d'un moment de rigueur,
Je n'ai pour lui parler consulté que mon cœur.
Et qui ne se serait comme moi déclarée
Sur la foi d'une amour si saintement jurée?
Me voyait-il de l'œil qu'il me voit aujourd'hui?
Tu t'en souviens encor, tout conspirait pour lui.
Ma famille vengée, et les Grecs dans la joie,
Nos vaisseaux tout chargés des dépouilles de Troie,
Les exploits de son père effacés par les siens,
Ses feux que je croyais plus ardents que les miens,
Mon cœur, toi-même enfin de sa gloire éblouie,
Avant qu'il me trahît, vous m'avez trahie.
Mais c'en est trop, Cléone, et quel que soit Pyrrhus,
Hermione est sensible, Oreste a des vertus,
Il sait aimer du moins, et même sans qu'on l'aime;
Et peut-être il saura se faire aimer lui-même.
Allons, qu'il vienne enfin.

CLÉONE   Madame, le voici.

HERMIONE   Ah! je ne croyais pas qu'il fût si près d'ici.

                                  (*Andromaque*, II, I)

This passage comes at the end of a scene in which Hermione has
expressed, and at times very violently, her awareness of contradictory feelings towards Pyrrhus. Here she recalls bitterly the
beginning of her love for him, and enumerates the reasons
which justified this love and her former hope. It is, of course,
the absurd logic of passion which looks for reasonable elements
in unreasonable feelings. Not one of the reasons given by Hermione, nor even the force of their number, could prove that
Pyrrhus was bound to reciprocate her love. But to Hermione,
as she conjures up, probably for the hundredth time, the complete picture of all the auspicious circumstances which surrounded her first meeting with Pyrrhus, the picture appears
unbearably convincing, even to the point of suggesting that
Pyrrhus was in fact at the time in love with her:

     Me voyait-il de l'œil qu'il me voit aujourd'hui?

So convincing that, if it were an illusion, it must have been an illusion cruelly engineered by everybody around her. Hence the suspicious 'tout conspirait', leading to the outburst 'vous m'avez tous trahie' and the impulse to strike at the nearest responsible person 'toi-même enfin'. At this point, against this hopeless background of universal treachery, Oreste appears as the only virtuous and reliable human being and, rejecting the fascination of Pyrrhus' glorious deeds 'et quel que soit Pyrrhus' (an ambiguous rejection which still preserves Pyrrhus' power of attracting her), she turns her thoughts towards Oreste. But the half-hearted quality of this move is immediately evident in her reluctance to see him.

Even this very rough analysis of the passage shows the kind of intimacy created between the character and the spectators. They have followed Hermione's building up of her case, perceived the apparent solidity of the past illusion as well as the lingering effects of this illusion in the present, felt the pressure of her mounting rage, the jerk when, after the outburst, weariness has prevailed, together with a need for something really solid to cling to, and measured the fragile and deceptive quality of this moment of good-will towards Oreste. The impression thus produced is the exact opposite to that produced by the workings of a mechanism, the nature of which is stiffness and regularity. Hermione's revelation of her state of mind possesses two attributes which we know, almost instinctively, to be the privilege of living human beings: the density of texture due to the complexity of the living mind; the warmth, suppleness and irregularity of the constant motion in any living organism. There is more: because we are so close to the living reality within the character, because we are so tied to the immediate feelings we share, we forget in a way that we know Hermione's ultimate doom. We are pulled in different directions and, in spite of our prescience, contemplate the possibility of things turning out differently. Racine, we know already, does not require the usual devices to provoke dramatic suspense. As I said in a previous chapter,[1] the spectators, well aware of the subsequent development of the plot, experience dramatic suspense vicariously through the characters. Part of their tragic emotion lies precisely in measuring the gap between the hero's present feelings and the clearly delineated course of destruction. But at the same time the gap appears incredible. The audience is made to live so intensely, so immediately the fears, hopes and illusions of the characters that future events seem improbable and uncertain compared with the actuality of the experience communicated. Paradoxically our personal curiosity as to the future is thus restored to us, not in the crude form of 'What is going to happen?' but as a more subtle and equally pressing question, 'How can it happen?'

The complexity of layers in the expression of the characters' feelings compels the spectator to experience, as in real life, some uncertainty as to the true colour of an emotion. Such is the effect of Néron's ambiguous statement, already mentioned in chapter 2,

J'aimais jusqu'à ces pleurs que je faisais couler.

At times the hero's own hesitations about the motivation of his feelings increase the impression of the human heart as an intricate blend of elusive reactions.

Thus Néron experiences some difficulty in assessing his deeper feelings towards his mother:

Mais (je t'expose ici mon âme toute nue)
Sitôt que mon malheur me ramène à sa vue,
Soit que je n'ose encor démentir le pouvoir
De ces yeux où j'ai lu si longtemps mon devoir;
Soit qu'à tant de bienfaits ma mémoire fidèle
Lui soumette en secret tout ce que je tiens d'elle,
Mais enfin mes efforts ne me servent de rien;
Mon génie étonné tremble devant le sien.

(*Britannicus*, ii, ii)

[1] Cf. chapter 3, pp. 37–39.

At the very moment when Néron reveals his 'âme toute nue', the revelation is not that of barren simplicity but of troubled depths, as yet imperfectly plumbed, where long-lived habits and reluctant feelings of gratefulness struggle with a will to revolt scarcely emerging, and still held back by something even deeper, the obscure almost magnetic power Agrippine's eyes exert over her son.

As for the violent oscillations which cause passion to light up, in rapid succession, utterly different corners of the human heart, their lifelike frenzy is particularly striking in Phèdre, when jealousy reveals the most extreme forms which desire for revenge, sense of guilt, panic and bitterness alike can assume within her. A few lines from the well-known speech 'Ils s'aimeront toujours' will recall the extraordinary mobility of Phèdre's thoughts:

> Au moment que je parle, ah! mortelle pensée!
> Ils bravent la fureur d'une amante insensée.
> Malgré ce même exil qui va les écarter,
> Ils font mille serments de ne se point quitter.
> Non, je ne puis souffrir un bonheur qui m'outrage,
> Œnone. Prends pitié de ma jalouse rage.
> Il faut perdre Aricie. Il faut de mon époux
> Contre un sang odieux réveiller le courroux.
> Qu'il ne se borne pas à des peines légères:
> Le crime de la sœur passe celui des frères.
> Dans mes jaloux transports je le veux implorer.
> Que fais-je? Où ma raison se va-t-elle égarer?
> Moi jalouse! Et Thésée est celui que j'implore!
> Mon époux est vivant, et moi je brûle encore!
> Pour qui? Quel est le cœur où prétendent mes vœux?
> Chaque mot sur mon front fait dresser mes cheveux.
> Mes crimes désormais ont comblé la mesure.
> Je respire à la fois l'inceste et l'imposture.
> Mes homicides mains, promptes à me venger,
> Dans le sang innocent brûlent de se plonger.
> Misérable! et je vis? et je soutiens la vue

De ce sacré Soleil dont je suis descendue?
J'ai pour aïeul le père et le maître des Dieux;
Le ciel, tout l'univers est plein de mes aïeux.
Où me cacher? Fuyons dans la nuit infernale.
Mais que dis-je? Mon père y tient l'urne fatale.   (IV, vi)

The realization, complete and unshakable, of the actuality and indestructible solidity of Hippolyte's and Aricie's mutual love conjures up a picture of the two lovers in league against her, and rage against this insulting hostility brings the temptation of self-pity ('Prends pitié de ma jalouse rage') together with a ruthless determination to destroy Aricie. A possible scheme offers itself to Phèdre and the indictment she proposes to put forward derives its force from her own conviction that 'le crime de la sœur passe celui des frères'. Therefore the decision to appeal to Thésée takes its definite shape in her mind: 'Dans mes jaloux transports je le veux implorer.' The very wording of this decision shatters the illusion of self-righteous anger, and the planned revenge suddenly reveals the criminal madness in herself, the monstrous disjointing of her relations with Thésée and Hippolyte. This flashing awareness of all-pervading evil is then an unbearable experience which affects her whole being, so that her next reactions are the violent and useless efforts of the cornered fighter, seeking every way out of herself and out of life. The frantic exploration of a desperate state of mind has thus carried Phèdre and the audience from the giddy heights of criminal folly to the depths of remorse, from the very core of her being—'je respire à la fois l'inceste et l'imposture'—to the immense expanse of an implacable sky and the dark country of the dead. And each sudden illumination has been experienced by Phèdre and by the spectator with that uncontrollable shock of pain which, in real life, always precedes, if only by half a second, any realization of a hopeless predicament.

Illustrations of this life-like quality can be found in every speech and every line. Racine has moreover used to the full that protean quality of human feelings which makes them, when checked, reappear in another guise as if they were endowed with a clever wit of their own. Thus, for instance, when Pyrrhus has decided to marry Hermione, his obsession with Andromaque comes to the surface again in an oblique way, pretending to be no more than a purely intellectual speculation:

> Crois-tu, si je l'épouse,
> Qu'Andromaque en son cœur n'en sera pas jalouse? (II, v)

In the same scene, a few lines further on, we perceive once more not only the conflicting attitudes in Pyrrhus but also the very movement of the passion rapidly throwing a disguise over itself:

> Je veux la braver à sa vue,
> Et donner à ma haine une libre étendue.
> Viens voir tous ses attraits, Phœnix, humiliés.

Because of this privileged knowledge the spectator has of the characters' feelings, he is ready to be hit at the same time as they are by what hurts them.

From the beginning of *Iphigénie*, he is aware of Agamemnon's complex feelings through the character's self-revelation. He knows among other things how Agamemnon has pictured to himself with some misgivings his glorious task of taking the Greeks to Troy:

> Moi-même (je l'avoue avec quelque pudeur),
> Charmé de mon pouvoir, et plein de ma grandeur,
> Ces noms de roi des rois et de chef de la Grèce
> Chatouillaient de mon cœur l'orgueilleuse faiblesse. (I, i)

Therefore, when Clytemnestre charges him with sacrificing his daughter only through ambition, using words which are an echo of his own,

> Cette soif de régner, que rien ne peut éteindre,
> L'orgueil de voir vingt rois vous servir et vous craindre,
>
> (IV, iv)

the audience immediately feels how deep the wound goes, all the deeper because they know, just as Agamemnon himself knows, that this is only half the truth and that the cruel thrust is both deserved and unfair.

Undoubtedly this extraordinary closeness which Racine establishes between the states of mind of his characters and the audience is the very centre of his art.

In the intense light projected by passion, Racinian heroes appear stripped of all protection, transparent and essentially vulnerable.

*

The second reason why Racine's heroes are so close to us is that they are flesh and blood. Transparent as they are to the spectators, they retain between each other the screen of their physical reality.

It is true that we know nothing of their physical appearance, in the way we usually conceive of the physical appearance of human beings: we are given no indication as to the colour of their hair or of their eyes. As always, Racine here uses stylization and focusing. The physical reality of his characters is limited to what, in our relations with others, are at the same time the most powerful and the most revealing signs of our feelings: the tone of the voice, the expression of the face, a gesture, a look, a shudder.[1] This stylization corresponds to what happens in real life. Passions do not lie constantly buried inside us; at the slightest provocation they tend to manifest themselves in the form of an emotion which is a physiological reaction: we blush, turn pale, shudder, cry; our heart misses a beat, we turn our head.

The use Racine makes of the physical reality of his characters varies according to the particular dramatic needs of each tragedy. In *Mithridate* the characters seem very much in control of their emotions. It is only exceptionally that Xipharès and Monime can read a threatening message on Mithridate's face,

[1] In connection with this aspect of Racine's art, see J. C. Lapp, *Aspects of Racinian Tragedy*, pp. 134–46, and also the essay 'Les Yeux de César' by Jules Brody in *Studies in Seventeenth Century French Literature* (Cornell University Press, 1962), which is more specifically concerned with *Britannicus*.

the revelation being the more dramatic in a man whose attitudes are shaped by a long practice of cunning. The general
impression in the play is that of an outward impassivity which
is in keeping with Monime's and Xipharès' self-control and the
icy atmosphere of family relationships.

On the contrary Phèdre's passion is given a strong physical
reality. Her first words in the play suggest the complete exhaus-
tion of her body:

> Je ne me soutiens plus, ma force m'abandonne.
> Mes yeux sont éblouis du jour que je revoi,
> Et mes genoux tremblants se dérobent sous moi. (I, iii)

It is important in the play that Phèdre's passion should appear
as an unfair and unexpected blow from Vénus, striking first at
her body even before she could consciously acknowledge the
nature of the attack:

> Je le vis, je rougis, je pâlis à sa vue;
> Un trouble s'éleva dans mon âme éperdue;
> Mes yeux ne voyaient plus, je ne pouvais parler;
> Je sentis tout mon crops et transir et brûler.
> Je reconnus Vénus et ses feux redoutables. (I, iii)

It is equally important, since a feeling of guilt is part of Phèdre's
tragic fate, that passion should appear to her in the form of a
fatal disease, poisoning her whole being and destroying her
from within.

However, the almost hieratical dignity of characters in
Mithridate and the violence of bodily disorder in *Phèdre* are
exceptional cases. As a rule Racine's art lies in using to the full,
not the physical reality of a human being but the awareness
others have of this reality. The awareness and the danger of
betraying oneself are the more intense because, as we know,
the relations between Racinian characters are essentially desperate and dangerous. Frustration also increases the feeeling of
tenseness caused by the physical presence. Those bodies which

will never touch seem to impose their reality more forcibly and to possess at times an almost mesmeric power.

As can be expected, the physical presence of Hippolyte is felt by Phèdre as a brutal shock:

> Le voici. Vers mon cœur tout mon sang se retire.
> J'oublie, en le voyant, ce que je viens lui dire.　(II, v)

The presence of Agrippine brings confusion in the mind of Néron:

> Sitôt que mon malheur me ramène à sa vue,
> Soit que je n'ose encor démentir le pouvoir
> De ces yeux où j'ai lu si longtemps mon devoir;
> Soit qu'à tant de bienfaits ma mémoire fidèle
> Lui soumette en secret tout ce que je tiens d'elle,
> Mais enfin mes efforts ne me servent de rien;
> Mon génie étonné tremble devant le sien.　(II, ii)

Titus, completely overcome by the presence of Bérénice, cannot reveal his decision to her:

> Sortons, Paulin; je ne lui puis rien dire.　(II, iv)

Athalie, when she sees Joas, is filled with an uncontrollable emotion which comes from facing, not the product of a dream, but the physical reality of the child:

> O ciel! plus j'examine, et plus je le regarde,
> C'est lui. D'horreur encor tous mes sens sont saisis. (II, viii)

Racine's characters are well aware of the fact that the human face can both hide and reveal the deepest feelings. The Racinian hero feels the physical presence of his interlocutor as a kind of opaque barrier which he must break through, and he watches for the vulnerable spot. Each is either the watcher, waiting intently for some external manifestations of concealed passion, or the watched, who knows that nothing will escape the searching and vigilant eye.

In *Andromaque* (IV, v), while Hermione is speaking to Pyrrhus,

the latter betrays his lack of attention by an almost imperceptible sign; for one second, perhaps, he has turned away his eyes
but in a flash Hermione has seen this revealing movement:

> Vous ne répondez point? Perfide, je le voi,
> Tu comptes les moments que tu perds avec moi!
> Ton cœur, impatient de revoir ta Troyenne,
> Ne souffre qu'à regret qu'un autre t'entretienne.
> Tu lui parles du cœur, tu la cherches des yeux.

Thésée, convinced of Hippolyte's guilt, cannot suppress his
reaction of wonder when the young man appears before him,
and has some difficulty in dismissing as an illusion the physical
evidence of Hippolyte's innocence—

> Ah! le voici. Grands Dieux! à ce noble maintien
> Quel œil ne serait pas trompé comme le mien?
> Faut-il que sur le front d'un profane adultère
> Brille de la vertu le sacré caractère?   (IV, ii)

—and his rejection of the truth, which is so luminously present,
is given an added flavour of dramatic irony in the two following
lines:

> Et ne devrait-on pas à des signes certains
> Reconnaître le cœur des perfides humains?

Bajazet offers many instances of these fierce encounters in
which the physical expressions of emotion assume an overwhelming importance. In this play everybody has to lie, to
wear a mask, to save his life or his love. Words cannot be
trusted. Roxane will not be satisfied with verbal statements
alone:

> Je veux que devant moi sa bouche et son visage
> Me découvrent son cœur,...   (I, iii)

Atalide is well aware of the value a single glance can take on in
the dangerous game she and Bajazet are playing with Roxane.
It may be used as an ultimate warning:

> D'un mot ou d'un regard je puis le secourir.   (I, iii)

It may also shatter the fragile edifice of pretence, the more so as Bajazet feels unable to disguise his feelings:

> Et ma bouche et mes yeux, du mensonge ennemis,
> Peut-être dans le temps que je voudrais lui plaire,
> Feraient par leur désordre un effet tout contraire;
> Et de mes froids soupirs ses regards offensés
> Verraient trop que mon cœur ne les a point poussés. (II, v)

Yet Roxane's passionate scrutiny of Bajazet's countenance may at times lead her to the wrong interpretation of a sigh. At the moment when she gives up her threatening tone, breaks down, and confesses the full extent of her love for him—

> Oui, je te le confesse,
> J'affectais à tes yeux une fausse fierté.
> De toi dépend ma joie et ma félicité. (II, i)

—Bajazet shows some sign of emotion, which immediately raises some hope in her:

> Tu soupires enfin, et sembles te troubler.
> Achève, parle. (II, i)

The moment of self-deception is short-lived, but uncertainty remains. Even Atalide can be deceived by the false interpretation of a facial expression, and Acomat's description of a meeting between Roxane and Bajazet provokes in her the violent tortures of jealousy:

> J'ai longtemps immobile observé leur maintien.
> Enfin, avec des yeux qui découvraient son âme,
> L'une a tendu la main pour gage de sa flamme;
> L'autre, avec des regards éloquents, pleins d'amour,
> L'a de ses feux, Madame, assurée à son tour. (III, ii)

In an atmosphere where deceptiveness has so many shades, truth can come out only in the form of the most violent physical reactions. Atalide's faint is significant. It leaves Roxane without doubt as to her rival's love for Bajazet and strongly suggests that this love is reciprocated.

It is perhaps in *Britannicus* that Racine has used the terrifying power and the vulnerability of the sense of sight in such a complex way as to produce an effect of almost unbearable tension; this is in the scene in which Néron compels Junie to tell Britannicus that she does not love him any more. The effect of tension is carefully prepared. Néron is aware of the disturbing effect his presence has on Junie, when they meet at the beginning of Act II, scene iii:

> Vous vous troublez, Madame, et changez de visage.
> Lisez-vous dans mes yeux quelque triste présage?

If Néron is thus disappointed in reading in Junie's face feelings which cannot please him, he is not going to give Britannicus the satisfaction of reading on the same face an expression of love. Junie, for her part, knows that it is next to impossible for her not to betray her feelings towards Britannicus just by her way of looking at him:

> Mes yeux lui défendront, Seigneur, de m'obéir.

Néron realizes as well as she does the intense significance of a single look, but he knows also his power as the watcher. All the dangerous eloquence and threatening acuity of a glance are dramatically summed up by Néron's warning:

> J'entendrai des regards que vous croirez muets.

Throughout the whole of the encounter between Junie and Britannicus (with Néron present and hidden) Junie's face and eyes are the focal point and the spectator is conscious of the increasing tenseness of the muscles in her face. She feels Néron's eyes on her, remembering his words:

> Madame, en le voyant, songez que je vous voi.

She feels Britannicus' eyes which try to meet her own and can read in them the urgent appeal for reassurance, the pained incredulity and the scornful bitterness:

> Quoi! même vos regards ont appris à se taire?
> Que vois-je? Vous craignez de rencontrer mes yeux?
> Néron vous plairait-il? vous serais-je odieux? (II, vi)

The end of the scene leaves the protagonists in a state of torture. Néron himself is agitated by an even stronger feeling of jealousy than before, having found that passion could express itself in a subtler way than in a look:

> Hé bien! de leur amour tu vois la violence,
> Narcisse: elle a paru jusque dans son silence. (II, viii)

The expression of our face, the look in our eyes, the intonation of our voice are basic manifestations of our feelings. It is noteworthy that Néron, who is a 'monstre naissant', still human, should at the beginning of the play betray his emotions through physical reactions:

> ...Néron, d'aussi loin qu'il me vit,
> Laissa sur son visage éclater son dépit, (I, i)

says Agrippine in the first act. For a long time he remains vulnerable to the eyes of those around him, angered by Junie's looks of dislike, daunted by his mother's presence.

At the end of the play, however, Néron's eyes are no longer those of a human being but those of a monster, cold and expressionless:

> Néron l'a vu mourir sans changer de couler.
> Ses yeux indifférents ont déjà la constance
> D'un tyran dans le crime endurci dès l'enfance. (v, vii)

It is not surprising that we should feel an intense pity for Racinian characters. Stripped by the total awareness we have of their feelings and at the same time retaining the warmth of their voices, the quickening of their pulses, and most of all the soft or hard sparkle of their eyes, they are as near to us and as immediately present as human beings can be. But this intimate link between them and the audience does not bring them down to the level of ordinary human beings. It is the other way round: the spectator is brought up to the level of those human beings, who are exceptional.

★

At this point one must remember one of the elements of tragedy mentioned at the beginning of this study. In a tragedy man opposes to the destructive forces a magnified image of himself. Tragic heroes have, therefore, that characteristic of being more powerful, nobler, stronger, more handsome than ordinary people. This is what gives to the emotions of terror and pity a particular quality, a sort of exaltation, because the suffering and the defeat take place at the highest possible level of the human condition.[1]

Racine's characters are exceptional beings through the very intensity of their passions, but Racine has also taken advantage of the tradition which requires that they should be important people, kings, queens, princesses, high priests.

The possibilities of enlargement which Racine saw in the historical setting have been mentioned in connection with his use of time and space. It is already obvious that history and legend play a large part in his tragedies. But it would be wrong to think that the Trojan War in *Andromaque,* or Rome in *Britannicus* and *Bérénice,* was a kind of superb backcloth for the private conflicts of the characters. No element in a Racinian tragedy is external to the central point or an irrelevant ornamentation.

Hermione is not a jealous and frustrated woman who incidentally happens to be a princess. She is fundamentally a princess, with all the pride, dignity and power of her rank. Far

---

[1] This is why, among other reasons, Anouilh's play *Antigone* is such a bad play. Of the essence of tragedy Anouilh has kept just the bare mechanism. His Antigone has none of the characteristics of nobility and grandeur one would expect from the tradition. In fact, she has all the vulgar silliness of a badly brought up child in a lower middle-class family. It is rather dishonest to have called her Antigone; Marie-Claire or Caroline would have been more in keeping with the personality of the heroine.

from pushing aside the royal quality of his characters, Racine
has used it to the full, to increase still further the tragic import
of every situation and every movement of passion.

One dramatic use of this quality is the contrast between the
power a man has in the world and his helplessness against the
disastrous effects of passion. Throughout the tragedy of
Mithridate, the audience is never allowed to forget that Mithridate is a giant of history. As he says to Monime, even if he
were completely defeated, he would still be someone whose
glory any king might envy:

> Quand le sort ennemi m'aurait jeté plus bas,
> Vaincu, persécuté, sans secours, sans Etats,
> Errant de mers en mers, et moins roi que pirate,
> Conservant pour tous biens le nom de Mithridate,
> Apprenez que suivi d'un nom si glorieux,
> Partout de l'univers j'attacherais les yeux,
> Et qu'il n'est point de rois, s'ils sont dignes de l'être,
> Qui, sur le trône assis, n'enviassent peut-être
> Au-dessus de leur gloire un naufrage élevé,
> Que Rome et quarante ans ont à peine achevé.　　　(II, iv)

Mithridate has complete power over his sons, over Monime
herself, as she has agreed to marry him. He has the outstanding
intellectual qualities and the vigour which have made him the
most redoubtable enemy of Rome. The plan he reveals to his
sons of attacking the Romans in Rome shows the extent of his
imagination and of his daring. His practice of cunning is that
of the great statesman. Moreover, even his body has a distinctive quality, as poison cannot harm it. And yet Mithridate is
destroyed by his passion for Monime. All the things he can do
with his power, his imagination, his statesmanship will only
increase the catastrophic effects of his love. He turns one of his
sons into a bitter and dangerous enemy; his other son becomes
for him the cause of a frantic struggle between hatred and
affection. His scheming power, used to wrench Monime's secret

from her, places her in a position where she can refuse to marry him. The qualities of the great conqueror prove worse than irrelevant when dealing with passion. Not only do they emphasize dramatically the hero's tragic helplessness but, by adding their tremendous impetus to the fatal course of frustrated love, they also precipitate the downfall of the hero.

With Athalie the case is slightly different, but it is as dramatic, if not more so. The turmoil of her feelings undermines her qualities of statesmanship. Before the play begins, she has been a very capable ruler, who had brought peace to Jerusalem, kept in check 'l'Arabe vagabond' and 'l'altier Philistin' and secured a useful alliance with Syria. Passion invades the political sphere and she is on the point of losing those qualities of vigour and decision which make her a queen, and of becoming an ordinary human being, a mere woman:

> Ce n'est plus cette reine éclairée, intrépide,
> ......
> Elle flotte, elle hésite; en un mot, elle est femme. (III, iii)

This tragic disintegration of her regal personality is made more terrifying and more pitiful by her shocked awareness of an unworthy change in her—

> ... Je serais sensible à la pitié? (II, vii)

—and by the indomitable pride with which to the very end she gives orders to those about her:

> Quoi? la peur a glacé mes indignes soldats?
> Lâche Abner, dans quel piège as-tu conduit mes pas!
> ABNER   Reine, Dieu m'est témoin...
> ATHALIE   Laisse là ton Dieu, traître,
> Et venge-moi. (v, v)

Then, obviously, the fact that characters are kings and rulers means that their individual fate may affect the fate of a great number of other men. The Racinian tragedy is concerned with conflicts in personal relations: 'Il ne s'agit point dans ma tragédie des affaires du dehors. Néron est ici dans son particulier et dans sa famille';[1] but Racine keeps the audience constantly aware that a single emotion can have tremendous consequences. He establishes such close connections between the personal life of the character and his political situation that the character cannot make a move without setting in motion forces that will change the lives of hundreds of people. As passion in Racine is an absolute value, a single movement of hope or despair may have, at any moment, the most appalling consequences, and its tragic significance is therefore magnified by the endless vistas of peripheral effects which will inevitably follow.

The characters are not blind to those consequences, but such is the ruthless violence of self-centred passion that the intrinsic portentousness of war and mass slaughter is used by the Racinian hero only to stress the desperate extent of his own passion.

Pyrrhus is ready to start a war to please Andromaque:

> Tous les Grecs m'ont déjà menacé de leurs armes;
> Mais dussent-ils encore, en repassant les eaux,
> Demander votre fils avec mille vaisseaux;
> Coutât-il tout le sang qu'Hélène a fait répandre;
> Dussé-je après dix ans voir mon palais en cendre,
> Je ne balance point,... (I, iv)

So is Oreste, for Hermione's sake:

> Hé bien! allons, Madame:
> Mettons encore un coup toute la Grèce en flamme. (IV, iii)

The political framework of the Roman Empire depends on Titus' decision. In *Britannicus* much depends on the personal life of Néron: Rome will experience the difference between the virtuous emperor whom Néron might have been and the evil madman who will brand her with all the stigma of crime and corruption before finally using her as the theatre for grim fireworks. From the beginning of *Bajazet* the spectators have been warned that 'les destins de l'empire ottoman' are at stake. In

---

[1] (Première) Préface to *Britannicus*.

Athalie the consequences of the conflict affect not only the destiny of the Jewish state, but also the whole future of Christianity.

These large far-off consequences of a character's decision are not the only way in which the dangerous implications of a sudden emotion are brought home to the spectators. Much nearer stand nameless men and women whose fate is precariously hanging on the movements of a passion. They never appear on the stage, but their invisible presence can be felt throughout the play.

A few lines spoken by Roxane conjure up all the inmates of the seraglio whose lives and souls are subject to her power:

> Cette foule de chefs, d'esclaves, de muets,
> Peuple que dans ses murs renferme ce palais,
> Et dont à ma faveur les âmes asservies
> M'ont vendu dès longtemps leur silence et leurs vies.
>
> *(Bajazet, II, i)*

In *Bérénice* the Senate and the Roman people are constantly mentioned. They surround the protagonists with quiet but tense expectation, coming nearer and nearer until it seems that at any moment they may become visible:

> PAULIN Seigneur, tous les tribuns, les consuls, le sénat
> Viennent vous demander au nom de tout l'Etat.
> Un grand peuple les suit, qui, plein d'impatience,
> Dans votre appartement attend votre présence. (IV, viii)

Agamemnon's tent is in the middle of the camp. The audience is made conscious first of the sleeping soldiers, then of the bustle of the army, waiting for the wind and for Agamemnon's decision.

If, on the one hand, Racinian characters are exceptional because they have the power to make history, they are exceptional also because they are the prisoners of history. Their noble rank is not only a source of danger to hundreds of other men, it is also for them the cause of a frustration unknown to ordinary people. The outstanding example is Titus:

> Pourquoi suis-je empereur? Pourquoi suis-je amoureux?
>
> (IV, vi)

In *Bérénice*, Racine has deliberately enlarged both the political power of Titus and the size of the Roman Empire. Titus is, as he says himself, 'maître de l'univers', and his calling as an emperor, which for him is an absolute value, is to be in charge of the world; as he says, when he reflects that he has not yet started his task:

> D'un temps si précieux quel compte puis-je rendre?
> . . . . . .
> L'univers a-t-il vu changer ses destinées?   (IV, iv)

Titus' position represents the highest responsibility a man can have, and so he towers above the world. 'L'univers fléchit à vos genoux,' Bérénice says to him. The central point of the play is the antithesis Rome–Bérénice. Therefore, Titus' passion for Bérénice, the other absolute value for him, partakes of the same quality of being boundless and supremely powerful. Both 'l'univers' and passion win at the end of the play, and the characters are destroyed as human beings. Their last gesture, which gives a harrowing depth to their parting and which also keeps the spectator at the highest level of the human condition, is to face the universe for the last time with a dignified implicit reproach:

> Adieu: servons tous trois d'exemple à l'univers
> De l'amour la plus tendre et la plus malheureuse
> Dont il puisse garder l'histoire douloureuse.   (V, vii)

History or legend, far from being a majestic background for the tragic, is combined with personal passion in the most intricate relationships. This intricacy is easily perceptible in Pyrrhus' famous conceit,

> Brûlé de plus de feux que je n'en allumai.   (I, iv)

His love for Andromaque is indeed something which consumes him entirely, and the metaphor is not an overstatement. The connection with the fire of Troy, caused by him, is loaded with meaning. It is as if Pyrrhus were desperately trying to rid himself of this historical past which stands between him and Andromaque, as if he considered that the suffering he undergoes because of his love more than compensated for the atrocities of war. The implications of this line are many: it underlines the irreducible nature of the obstacle between Pyrrhus and Andromaque, expresses the violence of his love, and gives a terrifying insight into the distortion of judgment wrought by the particular logic of passion.

The historical importance of Néron and Agrippine, their part as rulers, is also inextricably mixed with their relationship as mother and son. This comes out especially in scene ii of Act IV. The ambiguity of the tone has already been mentioned in this chapter. For the audience, listening to Agrippine's opening speech, it is impossible to distinguish between the reproachful moving tone of a mother and the cold cynicism of the Machiavellian politician.

In Roxane, the basic feature of passion, that is, the wish to enslave, is tightly connected with the political framework of Turkey. And this allows Racine to increase the ruthlessness of the tragic mechanism. In such a setting, where the destiny of an empire varies according to dramatic shifts from power to slavery and from slavery to power, shifts in opposite directions produced by every movement of passion assume the most frightening proportions.

★

It is because the historical or legendary side of the Racinian heroes is always so intimately linked with their personal passions that their double characteristic—to be at the same time so close to the audience and so distant—is a perfect blend and yet seems a paradox. At this point it may be noticed that the paradox is implied in the expression *héros moyen*, which is a contradiction in terms.

The paradoxical nature of Racine's heroes accounts for the tragic emotion felt by the audience being not only intense but complex, and including terror, pity and exaltation. Moreover, the choice of heroes such as Phèdre, Andromaque, Titus and Athalie provokes a feeling of strong anticipation. They come from distant and well-known regions of history and legend as familiar names and, it seems, unapproachable personalities. We have deep in us the half-formulated thought, 'Was this the face...?', and it is one of Racine's greatest achievements to have preserved in them that quality of beings from another race, the race chosen by history to represent mankind, while placing them so near to us that we can penetrate all their secrets and catch the tremor of their lips.

5

THE INTERPLAY OF ACTION
AND CHARACTERIZATION

In any good play, the plot—that is, the framework of incidents, simple or complex, upon which the drama is constructed—offers a basic unity and focuses the attention of the audience on a theme, or a character, or a group of characters. The famous rule of the unity of action, so much discussed in the seventeenth century,[1] represents a codification of dramatic techniques which tends to make the unifying process mechanically easier. A firm circle is drawn round the play, reducing to a minimum the intervention of chance and the possibility of further developments, so that, inside the circle, the dramatic action should be complete and self-sufficient. Moreover, all the succeeding episodes, main plot and secondary plots alike, must combine for a single purpose, and all must converge towards the centre of the circle, the ultimate point where the play ends. The geometrical nature of this ideal dramatic technique is reflected in the seventeenth-century French theatre, although, in the case of great dramatists like Racine, the unifying factor in the plot has to be found much deeper than in the mechanical observance of a ready-made pattern.

Racine certainly acknowledged his general approval of the pattern. In his preface to *Britannicus* he states the necessity of an orderly sequence in an action 's'avançant par degrés vers sa fin' and says of tragedy that 'étant l'imitation d'une action complète, où plusieurs personnes concourent, cette action n'est point finie que l'on ne sache en quelle situation elle laisse ces mêmes personnes'. But the perfection of his handling of his plots shows more concern with the individual

[1] For a full account of seventeenth-century theories on the unity of action, see Scherer, *La dramaturgie classique en France* (Paris, 1950), ch. v.

type of tragedy he was creating than with the niceties of contemporary theories.[1]

Since Racinian tragedy is essentially the fight between man and the passions which destroy him, the dynamic structure of the play must be such as to reveal the workings of stylized passion in the highest relief and to the exclusion of everything else. In the light of the preceding chapters it is easy to see that the relations between action and passion, even action and characterization, are bound to be extremely close. In fact, some aspects of Racine's dramatic technique, such as his handling of liaisons between scenes (which has been mentioned before), are part of the general organization that constitutes action.

It is well known that Racine took great pains in working out the outlines of his tragedies. The modifications he introduced in traditional plots and the combining of elements from different sources, as in *Phèdre*, are related to various other aspects of his tragedy, but are very much dictated by the necessity of presenting, as forcibly as possible, the rigorous pattern followed by destructive passion.

The mechanism of destruction must be shown as an organic whole, starting at the point when the dangerous forces are unleashed and without a break pursuing its course until the final catastrophe. It must work slowly enough for the spectators to follow the logical sequence of all the component moves and yet rapidly enough for them not to lose the sense of its relentless pressure. The complex, and even contradictory, nature of these requirements accounts for some of the most interesting and at time paradoxical features in the dramatic structure of a Racinian tragedy.

[1] This kind of perfection—or more exactly Racine's search for it—plays an important part in Professor Weinberg's *The Art of Jean Racine*. Although one may not always agree with Professor Weinberg's conclusions, the detailed study he has made of the structure of each successive tragedy brings out in the most fascinating way the kind of problem that each subject set for the dramatist and Racine's technical moves towards the perfect solution.

The first paradox is the part played by external events in what is essentially a 'psychological' tragedy. Indeed the sudden emergence of some outside force giving the initial impulse is made necessary by the very nature of the psychological element in Racine. Here we must remember that the feelings of Racinian characters possess a quality of timelessness and of constant intensity. The mechanism of destruction cannot be started by a change of heart or by any new element inside the minds of the characters, as is sometimes the case in Shakespeare: in *The Winter's Tale*, for instance, Leontes' unexpected and unmotivated outburst of jealousy starts the dramatic chain of events. Racinian heroes stand, so to speak, from the beginning of eternity, with all the potential catastrophic violence of their passions ready to explode. The provocation must come from outside and take the form of an external event: the gods ask Agamemnon to sacrifice his daughter; Titus' father dies; Oreste is sent to Pyrrhus by the Greeks.

One must immediately add that, although the device is necessary to set the mechanism of destruction going, the event and the circumstances are so rapidly integrated in what follows that they seem a part of the mechanism itself.

A very obvious case of this perfect integration is Néron's abduction of Junie. This brutal action is so much in keeping with what we soon learn about him that it appears more as a consequence than as a cause of his strained relations with his mother. It is also very much in keeping with the personality of Mithridate—the hero with a charmed life—that in that tragedy the passions of the other characters should come into the open with the news of his death; moreover, this false report seems to herald Mithridate's own technique of dissembling when, in Act IV, he pretends to free Monime from any obligation towards him in order to discover her feelings. In *Iphigénie*—a play in which the characters are closely related to the gods: Achille is 'fils d'une déesse'; Iphigénie, 'le pur sang du dieu qui lance le tonnerre'—it seems in the order of things that the occasion for the letting loose of passions, the oracle, partakes of the same divine origin as the heroes themselves. As has been remarked by some critics, the external event which sets the drama in motion strikes us, retrospectively, by its appearance of inevitability: the audience feels that Oreste was bound to come to Hermione, for one reason or another, and Pyrrhus to blackmail Andromaque.

External events are used also to complicate the working of the mechanism in the course of the play. The news of Thésée's death, which prompts Phèdre to confess her love to Hippolyte, is followed later by the news of his return, which gives further scope to the feeling of guilt in her and provokes the ultimate catastrophe. In the last act of *Mithridate* Arbate's ambiguous report on what is happening outside the palace brings to a paroxysm Mithridate's rage against his sons, against Monime, against the world at large, and reveals the full extent of Monime's love for Xipharès.

I have just mentioned the necessity for complications in the dramatic structure. This may sound surprising. One usually connects the action of a Racinian tragedy with the quality of extreme simplicity, and indeed quotations from the prefaces seem to support this view. In the preface to *Britannicus* Racine states his approval of 'une action simple, chargée de peu de matière', and in his preface to *Bérénice* he vigorously defends the simplicity of his subject. It is in a way true that Racine's tragedies have fairly simple plots—and this is particularly true of *Bérénice*—compared with the multiplicity of incidents and the number of secondary plots to be found in some other plays. But the bare and easy summary of the story is deceptive. In order to 'faire quelque chose de rien' (as Racine puts it in the preface to *Bérénice*), a dramatic superstructure must be added to the flat outline of the subject, and this superstructure may be far from simple. In fact Racine introduces complications to the dramatic movement of his tragedies whenever this is necessary to intensify the destructive power of passion within a character.

The best illustration of deceptive simplicity is *Bérénice*, the very play always given as the masterpiece of simplicity. The construction of the play is such that it slows down the mechanism of destruction in order to reveal the complex moves of passion. The alteration of the tempo, as well as the complexity of the characters' reactions, is made possible by the part ascribed to Antiochus, who is not only the 'confident monté en grade', as he has sometimes been called,[1] but has an important dramatic role as well as a tragic fate of his own. The complications produced by his relations with Titus and Bérénice are all directed towards a greater intensity of tragic emotion. The corroding ebb and flow of Titus' struggle and his hesitations are made more obvious by his use of Antiochus as a messenger to Bérénice. Bérénice's suffering on learning of Titus' decision to part from her is the more excruciating in that the blow is dealt twice—first by Antiochus, then by Titus himself—and is thus a more complicated and therefore more exquisite form of torture. The intricacies created by the three-cornered relationship bring into relief the slightest twist and turn in the hero's inner pursuit of his own destruction, even the false move into the blind alley of illusory hope:

> Rassurons-nous, mon cœur, je puis encor lui plaire:
> Je me comptais trop tôt au rang des malheureux.
> Si Titus est jaloux, Titus est amoureux.   (II, v)

Moreover, the characterization of Antiochus is built upon his love for Bérénice and this adds further dramatic moves which reveal yet another tragic effect of passion: the pitiless self-centredness which rules supreme in all the dialogues between Antiochus and Bérénice.

---

[1] This is Professor Raymond Picard's opinion in his short and brilliant introduction to the play in the Pléiade edition of Racine's works (p. 459). I must add that Professor Picard does not deny Antiochus' dramatic importance.

The dramatist's same wish to exploit dramatically the full range of a character's potential reactions accounts for Racine's borrowing from different sources when writing *Phèdre* and for his making Hippolyte in love with Aricie. Action is thus more complex than in Seneca or Garnier; Phèdre and Hippolyte also are the victims of a destructive force which attacks them from different angles: jealousy in Phèdre is added to her former torture and gives her one more cause for criminal thoughts and a harrowing feeling of guilt; Hippolyte is destroyed both as a consequence of Phèdre's love for him and of his own passion for Aricie. And here again one more aspect of the stylization of passion is shown, to emphasize its cruel predicament: the mutual love of Hippolyte and Aricie is as frustrated and as much doomed to annihilation as Phèdre's hopeless and guilty feelings.

Since the complications in the dramatic movement are thus closely connected with the characters and the relations between them, they vary in number and kind with each tragedy. *Bajazet* is probably the play to which the famous quotation 'une action simple, chargée de peu de matière' can least apply. In this play passion assumes particular features which require an elaborate combination of several forces at work. Roxane's ferocity, Bajazet's and Atalide's vulnerability, could only be exploited tragically with the support both of a complicated political setting and of a political plot running throughout the play. Acomat's tenacious scheming is closely interwoven with the devious manœuvres devised by Bajazet and Atalide to protect Bajazet's life and their love, and the equally devious course of Roxane's pursuit of Bajazet. Roxane's cruelty could not provoke tragic emotion in the audience if this side of her characterization were not complemented by other feelings in her. The spectators have to realize her own vulnerability, her obsession with the insecurity of her position, as well as the political conditioning which makes her conceive of human relations only in terms of master and slave; they have to witness her doubts and her anguish, and follow the desperate logic of a woman who exacts everything from the man she loves because she risks everything for him.

At the beginning of the play it is made clear that the dangerous relations between Roxane and Bajazet have been brought about by a complicated network of circumstances, and each of these will lead to further developments in the course of the play. The first two scenes, in which Acomat mentions what his wily tactics have already achieved, are significant as to the kind of incidents which are going to determine the sinuous outlines of the plot:

> Peut-être il te souvient qu'un récit peu fidèle
> De la mort d'Amurat fit courir la nouvelle.   (I, i)

> D'ailleurs un bruit confus, par mes soins confirmé,
> Fait croire heureusement à ce peuple alarmé
> Qu'Amurat le dédaigne,...   (I, ii)

Alarming reports, false or true, are the mainspring of the dramatic movement, creating a constant interplay of conjecture and shock, in an atmosphere of 'fausses confidences'—the most crucial false report being Amurat's inaccurate relation of the meeting between Roxane and Bajazet (II, iii), which provokes Atalide's jealousy. The misinterpretations and miscalculations which expose every facet of the characters' passions are well in keeping with the tragic climate of a play in which truth virtually has the part of the villain. We find the same complexity in the tempo of the dramatic movement which combines a slowing up of the mechanism (Acomat goes on scheming until the last minute; Atalide tries to exonerate Bajazet to Roxane, unaware that he is already dead) with an impression of extreme urgency.[1]

It may be possible to consider Racine's handling of the plot in *Bajazet* as an extreme example of complication; but there is

[1] For the acceleration of time at the end of *Bajazet*, see chapter 2, pp. 12, 22.

in every Racinian tragedy another form of complexity in the unfolding of the plot which is an essential part of the dramatist's technique.

As I have already said, a great deal of the dramatic intensity of the play comes from the fact that, although the audience perceives immediately the way in which every move inside a character's mind is going to affect another character, the latter may not at once be aware of it. The Racinian hero pursues his own line of thought, dictated by his passion, and goes on planning and hoping in the light of a previous situation. In Act v of *Britannicus*, when the audience knows that Néron, influenced by Narcisse, is no longer in a mood of docility towards his mother, Agrippine is still convinced that her conversation with him in Act IV has borne its fruit and, taking at its face value the display of affection he has lavished on her, she is full of confidence and triumphant pride:

> Il suffit. J'ai parlé, tout a changé de face. (v, iii)

Pyrrhus is not aware, when he leaves Hermione at the end of Act IV, that his conversation with her has sealed his fate. He does not register—as the spectators do—the threatening implications in Hermione's last words:

> Porte aux pieds des autels ce cœur qui m'abandonne;
> Va, cours. Mais crains encor d'y trouver Hermione. (IV, v)

Entirely wrapped up in his thoughts concerning Andromaque, feeling at last confident that she will marry him, he does not even pay any attention to Phœnix' warning:

> Seigneur, vous entendez. Gardez de négliger
> Une amante en fureur qui cherche à se venger. (IV, vi)

Tense with anticipation, deaf to everything, Pyrrhus can only say:

> Andromaque m'attend. Phœnix, garde son fils.

This is the last time he is seen, his face lit up with the certainty of happiness.

It is of course in the logic of the working of passion that each of the characters, obsessed by his own passion, should be momentarily blind and deaf to something which will inevitably affect that passion. Hence the delayed action of the mechanism on the characters and the effects of dramatic irony Racine thus achieves. Phèdre is so totally absorbed in her own guilty passion for Hippolyte that she has not taken into account the possibility of Hippolyte being in love with Aricie. Although, through her own experience, she ought to have known the power of Vénus over all human beings, she has relied on the young man's reputation for chastity:

> Je ne me verrai point préférer de rivale.   (III, i)

Dramatic irony is obviously a complex process in the presentation of action, and the staggering of tragic effects produced by the destructive mechanism modifies considerably the otherwise simple outline of the plot.

But, whatever the complexity of the dynamic structure in a Racinian tragedy, unity of action is preserved. As Scherer has rightly said, unity should not be confused with simplicity.[1] Unity of action is necessary in any good play, but the unifying elements vary very much from one form of drama to another. In Shakespeare, characters, sub-plots and incidents which seem disconnected are linked together through a common theme with, as a result, dramatic effects of contrasts and parallelisms. In Racine the mechanism of passion must be seen as a continuous movement. A secondary plot would distract the attention of the audience from the relentlessness of this mechanism; the

---

[1] 'La première et la plus fréquente des méprises qu'on rencontre au sujet de l'unité d'action résulte de la confusion de l'unité avec la simplicité. Pourtant une action n'est pas nécessairement simple: on dit qu'il y a de l'unité dans un ensemble quand les différentes parties qui le composent forment un tout' (*La dramaturgie classique en France*, p. 92).

whole tragedy depends on an unbroken logical sequence of events. There is no room for those incidents which are in some other tragedies a kind of illustration in a minor key of the major issue in the play (as, for instance, in Shakespeare's *Julius Caesar* the murder of Cinna, the poet, mistaken for Cinna, the plotter, illustrates the chaos following the assassination of a ruler). In Racine there is one major issue and the whole play is in a major key. Every tragedy is centred on one point, very clearly visible: will Andromaque agree to marry Pyrrhus, will Iphigénie be sacrificed, will Titus dismiss Bérénice from his life? The action in the play is made up of the conflicting attitudes of the characters, and all the feelings of all the characters converge towards the central point. Moreover, these attitudes are interdependent.[1] From *Andromaque* onwards Racine achieved the perfect dynamic pattern in which each reaction of a character affects immediately the situation of all the other characters.

The pattern can take different forms. The chain reaction in *Andromaque* is well known: any decision provoked by Andromaque's feelings affects Pyrrhus, Pyrrhus' decision Hermione, Hermione's Oreste. Andromaque is thus the pivot of the action. In *Bajazet* Bajazet plays the same part: every nuance in his attitude towards Roxane modifies instantly the situation and feelings of Roxane, Atalide and Acomat. The tightness of relationships increases the possibility of interaction between the characters: Acomat is given a personal interest in Atalide. The tightness is further increased when the relationship between two characters is a double one: Atalide is at the same time Roxane's rival and her accomplice in Roxane's love for Bajazet. An economical use of the confidants contributes also to the compactness of the dramatic network, as in *Britannicus*, where

[1] In his earlier tragedies, *La Thébaïde* and *Alexandre*, Racine did not reach this tightness of structure. The feelings of some of the characters tend to stray from the central point and the characters appear divided into groups.

Narcisse is both Néron's confidant and that of Britannicus, and Burrhus advises both Agrippine and Néron.

The close links which exist between the characters were mentioned in a previous chapter. When we remember also that many of Racine's tragedies are within the family circle, it is tempting to say that unity of action is the inevitable result of such relationships. But this would not do full justice to the perfection of Racine's unifying technique.

It is not enough to say that action in Racine is composed of successive steps following logically towards one ultimate conclusion, within a pattern of interconnected passions. In fact the idea of successive steps is inaccurate, as it gives the impression that certain scenes, certain words uttered by the characters, mark a progression in the development of the plot, whereas in a Racinian tragedy every line, every word is part of the action. When analysing the quality of living human beings in Racine's heroes, I stressed the fact that they present us not with static feelings, but with passion alive, and therefore constantly moving. Even a long speech is essentially a movement of action. For Racine anything which is not necessary to the action of the tragedy should be cut out: 'On ne peut prendre trop de précaution pour ne rien mettre au théatre qui ne soit très nécessaire. Et les plus belles scènes sont en danger d'ennuyer du moment qu'on peut les séparer de l'action, et qu'elles l'interrompent au lieu de la conduire vers la fin.'[1]

There are no conversations between characters whose feelings cannot directly affect the feelings of each other. In *Andromaque* Oreste and Andromaque never meet. There is no exchange of views between characters who are not personally involved in the action, for the very good reason that there are no onlookers. The confidants are dramatic tools whose main function is to give a convenient structure to the heroes' inner monologues. They are not allowed to detach themselves from

[1] Préface to *Mithridate*.

this function, to stand back and express a personal opinion. The opinions they voice are limited to what illuminates the movements of passion in the main characters. There is no chorus to comment on the characters' actions with philosophical detachment, except in *Athalie* and *Esther*. And even then the role ascribed to the chorus in *Athalie* is, as we shall see, that of delineating the framework of the Christian order. The choruses do not constitute a break in continuity in the dynamic pattern, as they scarcely mention the protagonists or the tragic conflict; the general themes of their religious lyrics belong to a different plane from that of the tragedy proper. In *Esther* the chorus steps down on to the plane of the protagonists, and their comments on the situation or on the characters certainly lessen the tension. However *Esther* is not really a tragedy but a poem written in a dramatic form in which Racine is more concerned with praising God's ways than with expressing tragically the destructiveness of passions.[1]

★

If action is conditioned by the psychology of the characters, the reverse is equally true. Characterization is influenced by the dramatic movement of the play.[2]

While considering the stylization of passion in the Racinian tragedy, I have already shown to what extent the feelings of the characters were streamlined and selected so as to suit the mechanism of destruction. But I was concerned with psychological aspects common to all Racinian heroes, whereas characterization implies the existence of individual features in particular characters.

One might think that the stylization of psychology would

[1] See below, chapter 6, p. 131.

[2] This aspect of Racine's art is given a central part in Professor Weinberg's book, *The Art of Jean Racine*, and I am very much in agreement with him on this point. His demonstration, based on detailed and exhaustive analysis, is most convincing, although it leaves out, to my mind, some other and most important components of the Racinian hero's personality.

debar Racinian heroes from having a strong individuality. All the features which in ordinary life enable us to form a picture of a man's personality—degree of intelligence or imagination, tastes, special gifts, and so on—are absent. The physical appearance of the characters is equally stylized and does not include any idiosyncrasies.

It is not absurd to suppose that extreme stylization might lead to the complete irrelevance of characterization. In fact, this is more or less what happens in Marivaux's theatre, where the characters are scarcely differentiated, with the result that all his heroines, and all his heroes, are practically interchangeable. In Racine, however, in spite of stylization, the audience is strongly aware of the individuality of the characters. Nobody would equate Roxane with Hermione and even the young heroes, such as Bajazet, Britannicus or Hippolyte, who all seem to fall within the same type of innocent victim, are very different from one another.

This individuality greatly strengthens the bond of sympathy between the spectators and the hero; it gives to the tragic experience they witness that characteristic of uniqueness which they personally know to be in real life the hallmark of any intensely felt experience.[1] As is always the case in Racine, this individualization of the characters is not a quality superimposed on them but remains strictly functional and depends very much on the place the character occupies in the whole structure of the play. Each distinctive feature is part of a complex system of relations and does not exist for its own sake, although the result is to give the audience the impression of the complete distinct personality of the hero.

Several elements come into play, all necessary to the complete structure of the tragedy: the particular legendary or historical

---

[1] Marivaux, in writing comedies, did not require this emotional bond between audience and characters since, in a comedy, the audience should, on the contrary, remain detached and view the play intellectually.

quality of the character (a necessary feature of the *héros moyen*), his relevance in some cases to the moral order which, as we shall see later, is an important element in tragedy, and, what is more particularly my concern here, the requirements of the action. At the same time, these various elements form a harmonious whole and are such that the individuality of a hero never prevents him from embodying the general characteristics of stylized passion.

Pyrrhus and Oreste both illustrate man's destruction through the same logical mechanism of passion. But some aspects of the working of the mechanism are more emphasized in Pyrrhus and others in Oreste, and the differentiation between them is closely related to the different parts they play in the development of the action.

One general feature of passion is the instability of the states of mind it creates. Pyrrhus is presented to us as 'un cœur si peu maître de lui':

PYLADE Il peut, Seigneur, il peut, dans ce désordre extrême,
Épouser ce qu'il hait, et punir ce qu'il aime.   (I, i)

As Professor Weinberg remarks,[1] this instability in Pyrrhus is dramatically important, as Pyrrhus is the nearest character to Andromaque on whom the dramatic action depends. He must be such as to react violently to every move of Andromaque and also to offer her with brutal clarity the alternative: marriage or the death of her son. Therefore Pyrrhus appears to us as the man of sudden fits of rage and sudden moments of ecstasy, constantly moved by the extremes of antithetical feelings. He says to Andromaque:

Songez-y bien: il faut désormais que mon cœur,
S'il n'aime avec transport, haïsse avec fureur;   (I, iv)

and again in his last conversation with Andromaque:

[1] *The Art of Jean Racine*, p. 74 ff., where the dramatic function of Pyrrhus and Oreste is analysed in a more detailed way than I can do in the present study.

Et là vous me verrez, soumis ou furieux,
Vous couronner, Madame, ou le perdre à vos yeux.

(III, vii)

The violent oscillations of his thoughts account easily for the resolution he takes in Act II to marry Hermione, at a moment when he is angered by his last (off-stage) conversation with Andromaque.

The impulsive brutality, the fiery temperament, are also connected in Pyrrhus with an important element in the structure of the play: the Trojan War. He himself acknowledges his excessive cruelty in the war:

Madame, je sais trop à quels excès de rage
La vengeance d'Hélène emporta mon courage;   (IV, v)

and he remains in Andromaque's mind the pitiless warrior, exulting in the sinister glow of blazing palaces:

Figure-toi Pyrrhus, les yeux étincelants.   (III, viii)

To Hermione, who mentions his exploits several times, he is like some god of war, of that Trojan War which is still so much in the minds of all the characters.

This kind of sanguine vitality in Pyrrhus permeates also his passion for Andromaque, and the obsessional characteristic of passion assumes in him the form of a kind of physical tenseness, almost of ecstatic trance, clearly perceived by the audience whenever the rest of the world becomes completely obliterated for him by the near presence of Andromaque:

Une autre fois je t'ouvrirai mon âme:
Andromaque paraît   (I, iii)
Andromaque m'attend...   (IV, vi)

The two sides of Pyrrhus' character, his outbursts of fiery love and his outbursts of fiery rage, merge completely in the conceit:

Brûlé de plus de feux que je n'en allumai,   (I, iv)

which is also a dramatic statement, as it relates to the central motivation of the play: Andromaque's memory of Troy and

Pyrrhus' refusal to face the fact that Troy stands for ever between Andromaque and himself.

The dramatic function of Oreste is very much in evidence at the beginning and end of the play. At first a passive instrument of fate, he starts the mechanism of tragedy by his arrival in Epire; he becomes later an active agent of destruction through the murder of Pyrrhus. Characterization is very closely related to this double function; certain sides of frustrated passion are emphasized in him from the beginning: a kind of hopelessness born of a long sequence of despairing moments—

> ...et tu m'as vu depuis
> Traîner de mers en mers ma chaîne et mes ennuis. (I, i)

—and the sense that, whatever he might do to take Hermione back to Greece, he is not in control of the situation:

> Je me livre en aveugle au destin qui m'entraîne. (I, i)

He thus acknowledges himself a docile tool for any forces which will drive him—and, what he does not realize, will drive others as well—he knows not whither. The despair which at times accompanies frustrated passion is in Oreste a permanent state leading to an obsession with death. This death-wish is mentioned by his friend Pylade in the first scene:

> Je craignais que le ciel, par un cruel secours,
> Ne vous offrît la mort que vous cherchiez toujours;

and by Oreste himself in his first meeting with Hermione:

> J'ai mendié la mort chez des peuples cruels
> Qui n'apaisaient leurs Dieux que du sang des mortels. (II, ii)

Two other features are also very clearly indicated: his complete dependence on Hermione's feelings:

> J'aime; je viens chercher Hermione en ces lieux,
> La fléchir, l'enlever, ou mourir à ses yeux; (I, i)

and the suggestion that his melancholy may endanger his reason, this suggestion being reinforced in the course of the play by references to his 'aveuglement funeste' and 'fureur extrême'.

Characterization here represents a very economical selection of those aspects of passion which, by a logical development, will lead to the murder of Pyrrhus and the inner destruction of Oreste himself.

The transition from a passive and reluctant abdication of self-will to a compulsive wish for desperate action is easily perceived by the audience, although it does not imply any volte-face in Oreste. From the beginning there is in him an ill-defined intimation that he may be compelled to some violent act: La fléchir, *l'enlever*, ou mourir à ses yeux.

The growth of irresistible impulses in him reaches a climax in Act III when, speaking to Pylade, he justifies them rationally, finding them in keeping with the general picture of the world:

> Mon innocence enfin commence à me peser.
> Je ne sais de tout temps quelle injuste puissance
> Laisse le crime en paix et poursuit l'innocence.
> De quelque part sur moi que je tourne les yeux,
> Je ne vois que malheurs qui condamnent les Dieux.
> Méritons leur courroux, justifions leur haine,...   (III, i)

This is the point at which he becomes an active, willing and conscious agent of the destructive forces of tragedy. The state of mind revealed here is not only related to the development of the plot; undoubtedly it leads to the murder of Pyrrhus, but it is also a statement on the tragic condition of man and is, significantly, an indictment of the gods.[1] In this respect it adds to the stature of Oreste as a tragic hero. What is also added to the personality of the character is the suggestion of his future destiny. The passage conjures up the rational form his madness will take. In the sinister inner world where an

>   ...injuste puissance
> Laisse le crime en paix et poursuit l'innocence,

---

[1] The part played by the gods in Racinian tragedy will be examined in the next chapter.

he will be the doomed avenger, killing his criminal mother in a vain attempt to restore justice in the universe, against the gods.

At the end of the play Oreste is charged by Hermione with full responsibility for Pyrrhus' and her own destruction. He is denounced as the initial cause of the tragedy:

C'est toi dont l'ambassade, à tous les deux fatale,
L'a fait pour son malheur pencher vers ma rivale; (v, iii)

and his senseless, unprofitable murder of Pyrrhus has brought the final catastrophe. The tragic irony of his own destruction is that the hero who has been constantly begging for death will not die but will be for ever a prey to madness and the tortures of frustrated passion.

Thus the personality of Oreste emerges clearly and forcibly. His dramatic function is comparatively simple, although very important. We are given all the nuances of the movements which ineluctably make him murder Pyrrhus. But through these nuances the character is enriched beyond his purely dramatic value, as they are connected with other elements in the structure of the tragedy. As a result his individuality assumes an almost symbolic value. He remains for the audience the tragic hero *par excellence*, standing on the doubtful frontier which separates ill-luck from responsibility, his cruel doom an apposite illustration of the classical *quem deus vult perdere, prius dementat*.

Some Racinian characters have a complex dramatic function, and their personality is accordingly made up of various facets which, while required by the necessities of the plot, possess at the same time a particular degree of significance in the whole structure of the play.

The individuality of a character like Néron is very much related to the complicated network of relations on which depends the dramatic movement that leads to the death of Britannicus. In his case characterization has a particular thickness of texture, made even richer by references to Néron's historical past and future woven into the warp of his present feelings. Frustration in him springs from several causes: his inferiority complex towards his mother, the previous efforts of his 'trois ans de vertus', his love for the virtuous Junie. Accordingly, his attitude to those around him is far from simple. Even his relations with Burrhus could not be summed up as the dwindling respect of a former pupil for a wise master. Certainly Néron sees in Burrhus a troublesome reminder of the virtuous path; but he sees him also as possessing political acumen and as an ally against his mother, while, quite rightly, denying him any understanding of the passion of love.

The various components of Néron's character are even more obvious in his dealings with Junie and Agrippine. His love for Junie has all the characteristics of total passion, including the shock of discovery, the feeling of a deep alteration in oneself and the overwhelming certainty of a lifelong commitment:

> Narcisse, c'en est fait, Néron est amoureux.
> . . . . . .
> Depuis un moment, mais pour toute ma vie
> J'aime (que dis-je aimer?), j'idolâtre Junie.   (II, ii)

The content of these lines and the tone, which expresses an almost naïve exultation, leave no doubt as to the genuine nature of Néron's love. At the same time his love for Junie is coloured by nuances which derive from the complexity of his frustration. Junie's reputation for virtue has prompted him to abduct her, and the irritating fascination this virtue has for him is part of his feelings, the more irritating as it ties in so naturally with the lingering thought of his own 'trois ans de vertus'. Everything is an obstacle to his passion:

> Tout: Octavie, Agrippine, Burrhus,
> Sénèque, Rome entière, et trois ans de vertus;   (II, ii)

and although the main cause of Néron's frustration is Junie's own feelings, all these other elements contribute to create in him the desperate urge to call up all the resources of his mind. First is conceit:

> Mais je m'en fais peut-être une trop belle image;
> Elle m'est apparue avec trop d'avantage:
> Narcisse, qu'en dis-tu? (II, ii)

Soon follow more dangerous features: the cynical self-assurance which assumes that the gods are on his side and not on the side of Octavie:

> Les Dieux ne montrent point que sa vertu les touche: (II, ii)

and the growing cruelty and sadism which come to the surface with

> Je me fais de sa peine une image charmante. (II, viii)

If, on the one hand, Néron's passion for Junie reveals conflicting impulses in him and alarming tendencies, his character depends also on the way it affects Agrippine: the frightening features which she discovers in him are in fact her own ambition, cunning and ungratefulness. Néron confronts her with the very means of achieving his ends which she herself has used, as well as with the impending failure of all that she has done. Both are prisoners of a tradition of corruption, the historical setting which she has contributed to create, while she clings to the illusory relationships between a devoted mother and a docile son. This setting, which gives such sombre depths to the relationship between them, accounts for what in the character of Néron has been called his 'cabotinage', his taste for histrionics. Rome has become a place where only appearance counts and truth is discredited or irrelevant. When Agrippine threatens Burrhus that she will reveal all her crimes publicly, Burrhus retorts that such a confession would be considered a political manœuvre and nobody would believe her. To Néron all the world's a stage; at first a spectator watching the arrival of Junie at the palace, he soon becomes the producer, staging the cruel meeting between Junie and Britannicus, and finally the main actor, his remarkable gifts for elaborate performance reaching a sinister perfection in his display of filial love and in his whole attitude during the banquet. Two instances of his superb play-acting are given indirectly through Agrippine and Burrhus, so that we have a full picture of Néron's acting, which includes his gestures and facial expressions.

The intricacies in the dramatic part played by Néron in the tragedy combine admirably with the historical framework, with the atmosphere of a corrupt and decadent Rome, and they give the Racinian Néron a distinctive personality. They stamp even the most stylized manifestations of his physical being with a special character which we recognize as his own: the sulky face, the shifty eyes in front of Agrippine, the cruel stare while watching Junie, and the hypocritical demonstrations—

> J'embrasse mon rival, mais c'est pour l'étouffer (IV, iii)

—and also something else, more elusive: the youthfulness of the face.

This kind of individualization is not the monopoly of the major characters, and one must not assume that the young men and women who have minor parts are less differentiated and can be simply described as victims.

The word victim is in any case partly misleading, as it implies a passivity which is not to be found in any of these characters. The passion of love is present in Hippolyte and that of ambition in Achille, and they are fundamentally the same passions, total and frustrated, as those to be found in Phèdre or Agamemnon. The reason why we tend to consider them as minor characters is that the light thrown by the dramatist on the tragic situation is not focused on them. Although their position in a given tragedy may not appear a central one, it is nevertheless an essential component of the whole structure, and this position gives each of them a very distinct personality.

Racine's Hippolyte may appear at first a pale image of the Hippolyte we meet in the classical dramatists and in Garnier. The legendary adjuncts of his hunting, horse-taming, out-of-door life are reduced to a minimum and even presented negatively. His companions have vanished; even his fierce chastity has been taken away from him. Yet the Racinian Hippolyte has a very definite personality, but the essence of the character is determined by Phèdre's passion for him. What is emphasized is his innocence, a kind of luminous innocence:

> Le jour n'est pas plus pur que le fond de mon cœur. (IV, ii)

The fact that Phèdre is in love with innocence makes her love even more hopeless and therefore more tragic. Until Act IV, Hippolyte for her is chastity as well as innocence and, as such, painfully removed, but at least there is left to her the bitter-sweet comfort that the impossible dream was all her own. With her discovery of Hippolyte's love for Aricie, innocence is no longer an aura of subtle grace round Hippolyte's supposed indifference to women; it becomes the positive, triumphant and insulting quality of the love which exists between him and Aricie:

> Hélas! ils se voyaient avec pleine licence.
> Le ciel de leurs soupirs approuvait l'innocence;
> Ils suivaient sans remords leur penchant amoureux;
> Tous les jours se levaient clairs et sereins pour eux. (IV, vi)

The contrast between this innocence and the constant atmosphere of guilt in which she lives brings Phèdre's tortures to the point where only the prospect of action can afford some relief:

> Non, je ne puis souffrir un bonheur qui m'outrage. (IV, vi)

The pattern of the play is that the guilt of Phèdre moves constantly forward until she gives in to the worst movement of all, and the one most deadly to her love and to herself—

> ...opprimer et noircir l'innocence! (III, iii)

—whereas innocence, as if frightened by the intimation of destruction and completely helpless, moves constantly backwards. Hippolyte's only salvation seems to be in flight. This is perhaps why some readers are tempted to see in him a weak young man, pathetically unfit to deal with the situation. Such a view is a very crude effort to bring the character down to the level of irrelevant average standards of behaviour. Hippolyte's movements are part of the dynamic structure of the play.

From the beginning he means to go away:

> ... je pars, cher Théramène,
> ......
> Et je fuirai ces lieux que je n'ose plus voir. (i, i)

This first scene, in which Hippolyte feels guilty for being in love with an enemy of his father, underlines the fastidious nature of his innocence as well as a semi-instinctive unwillingness to come near Phèdre.

After the terrible confession, his reaction is again to flee:

> Théramène, fuyons... (ii, vi)

When accused by his father, his attitude is significant. He does not fight back, except with the statement of his basic innocent nature. The only weapon of innocence is the glaring evidence of its existence. Up to the end, when he decides to go away with Aricie, Hippolyte never questions the absolute value of this innocence which, by its very nature, ought to escape destruction:

> Mais l'innocence enfin n'a rien à redouter. (iii, vi)
> Sur l'équité des Dieux osons nous confier. (v, i)

The character of Hippolyte is thus mainly determined by Phèdre's passion, and he appears as essentially marked by this quality of innocence which endows him with a particular kind of radiance, and by the tragic paradox attached to this innocence, which gives him such power over Phèdre's heart while at the same time being the very core of his vulnerability.

The innocence of Britannicus is different. In a setting of plots, dissimulation, secret actions, Britannicus stands for frankness and expects frankness. He knows that the court is corrupt, but his character is such that he must trust somebody. He complains to Narcisse that he is surrounded by spies and badly armed against them. (Such a flash of awareness is particularly ironical, as it is confirmed by what we know of the man in whom he confides.) This trusting nature makes him particularly vulnerable in the scene where Junie averts her eyes, knowing that Néron is watching them, and it later causes him to go to the banquet with the illusion that everything is well. His last meeting with Junie reveals in full the strength of his own outlook on men and life. He trusts Agrippine and Burrhus:

> Je m'en fie aux transports qu'elle m'a fait paraître;
> Je m'en fie à Burrhus;...   (v, i)

because he quite rightly considers that it is in their interest to support him. He trusts Néron because he interprets Néron's reactions in the light of his own open heart:

> Je crois qu'à mon exemple impuissant à trahir,
> Il hait à cœur ouvert, ou cesse de haïr;   (v, i)

and he trusts Narcisse because, for Britannicus, any man is presumed innocent until one has proof of his crime:

> Et pourquoi voulez-vous que mon cœur s'en défie?   (v, i)

His frankness is something positive, even aggressive, as can be seen by the way in which he stands up to Néron in Act III, scene viii, each of his remarks a vigorous thrust, aimed at Néron's most vulnerable sides. For a brief moment the evil in Néron is ironically exposed, the hopelessness of his love for Junie derisively underlined; and Néron is reduced to physical violence. Even when Britannicus finds himself arrested by the guards and prevented from fighting any more, his last sarcasm asserts his superiority over his opponent:

C'est ainsi que Néron sait disputer un cœur.   (iii, viii)

His character stands as an antithesis to Néron and to Néron's court. In this play, which is steeped in the rottenness of a decadent society, Britannicus is the embodiment of healthy vigour, fairness in love and war, and spirited daring.

Racine's innocent heroines, Junie, Aricie, Iphigénie, Atalide, Monime, are, in the same way, very different from one another, and their individuality is determined by the dramatic action as well as by various other functional elements in the general structure of the plays. Junie's virtue is the main cause of Néron's tragic destruction; she also stands for the moral values which will win in the end, and therefore the personality of the heroine is marked by mature poise, a faculty of clearsightedness, and a quiet refusal of any compromise. On the other hand, Atalide is deeply involved in all the lies which constitute the action of *Bajazet*; this function gives her complex reactions and accounts for the features of restlessness so prominent in her. This restlessness, or even agonizing aimlessness, is equally determined by the particular atmosphere of the play. Whereas Iphigénie is, cruelly and firmly, encircled by the framework of family relations and Monime's outlook is clearly delineated by an exquisite code of self-respect, Atalide lives in a world of uncertainties where courageous exploits are just ghostly shades of the past and the only positive order is the evil rule of the sultan.

There remains to be mentioned a group of characters whose individuality is more precarious: the confidants. They were a theatrical convention; their original function was to act as messengers bringing a fresh piece of news and to give the main characters an opportunity to express their feelings. The part confidants play in Racine is very much in keeping with the convention, but they possess certain characteristics more closely related to the structure of a Racinian tragedy, and the degree of individuality they may have is as carefully calculated as that of the main characters.

An obvious feature of the confidant is that there is no bond of sympathy between him and the audience, and what he says interests the spectator only in so far as it provokes a reaction from the hero. Racine has given to this negative feature a positive function: that of providing an illuminating antithesis between the universe of passion and the world outside, represented by the confidant. Paradoxically, the outsider lives in a state of complete symbiosis with the hero and is in the privileged position of having all the evidence at first hand, but this evidence he will interpret according to the pattern of a world which ignores the mechanism of passion. Therefore, the opinion he expresses, the advice he ventures to offer, will appear tragically irrelevant. The confidant may be the hero's best and most devoted friend, but nothing underlines more the fundamental loneliness of passion than the unbridgeable gap between the confidant's views and the character's feelings.

To the uncompromising nature of Racinian love the confidant opposes the alien ideal of a *juste milieu*, as when Céphise suggests to Andromaque that her faithfulness to Hector should remain within reasonable limits:

> Madame, à votre époux c'est être assez fidèle:
> Trop de vertu pourrait vous rendre criminelle.   (III, viii)

The confidant is always eminently reasonable, and this enables him to take an optimistic view of the crisis. We can measure the gap between his logic and the logic of passion in Arsace's efforts to comfort Antiochus:

> A ses pleurs accordez quelques jours;
> De ses premiers sanglots laissez passer le cours:
> Tout parlera pour vous, le dépit, la vengeance,
> L'absence de Titus, le temps, votre présence,

Trois sceptres que son bras ne peut seul soutenir,
Vos deux Etats voisins, qui cherchent à s'unir.
L'interêt, la raison, l'amitié, tout vous lie.   (III, ii)

This is a powerful enumeration of irrelevant arguments, stressing, negatively, all the aspects of Racinian passion which contradict Arsace's reasoning. Neither time nor space can affect Bérénice's feelings; passion is blind to worldly interests and to reason, and leaves no room for such mild sentiments as friendship.

This discrepancy between two worlds, two ways of looking at human relations, emphasizes with subtle irony the tragic predicament of the hero and perhaps nowhere so much as when the confidant assumes that passion can be curbed by willpower:

Il faut d'un vain amour étouffer la pensée,
Madame. Rappelez votre vertu passée.
(Œnone to Phèdre, III, iii)
On n'aime point, Seigneur, si l'on ne veut aimer.
(Burrhus to Néron, III, i)
Et qu'un héros vainqueur de tant de nations
Saurait bien, tôt ou tard, vaincre ses passions.
(Paulin to Titus, II, ii)

As representatives of an anonymous body of opinions which all run counter to the reality of passion, confidants have no individuality. But some of them are more actively connected with the destructive forces of tragedy, whether to help or to impede the mechanism of passion. As such they fulfil a specific purpose in a given play and derive from it some kind of individualization.

The individual features are limited to what is necessary to the dramatic structure and may amount to little. Thus Titus' confidant, Paulin, stands out among the other confidants only because he represents not the point of view of common sense but the opinion of Rome on the problem of Titus' marriage to a queen. This gives him a dignified stature and, beneath the respectful attitude of the confidant, the quiet self-assurance of the man who speaks in the name of Roman history, the Roman people and the Roman Senate. This is very much in evidence when, at the end of Act IV, while Antiochus presses Titus to go without delay to Bérénice, Paulin, boldly and sternly, puts forward Rome's rightful claims:

PAULIN   Venez, Seigneur, passons dans la chambre prochain:
          Allons voir le Sénat.
ANTIOCHUS   Ah! courez chez la Reine.
PAULIN   Quoi! vous pourriez, Seigneur, par cette indignité,
          De l'Empire à vos pieds fouler la majesté?
          Rome...   (IV, viii)

This is still, however, a vicarious kind of individuality. Confidants like Œnone, Burrhus or Narcisse, on the other hand, have a definite personality. But here again the individual characteristics are firmly restricted, although they may be effective in giving the impression of a character existing in his own right.

The restrictions are particularly interesting in the case of Œnone. The character was an integral part of the traditional legend, and in Racine, as in previous plays, is dramatically most important. But whereas, in some of the past tragedies, particularly in Garnier's *Hippolyte*, Phèdre's nurse had a rich and chaotic personality, the characterization of Racine's Œnone is carefully built up according to a coherent and comparatively simple pattern.

The link between the main character and the confidant is closer than in any other play, as Œnone's devotion to Phèdre knows no bounds; yet the gap between the confidant and the hero is nowhere so tragically obvious. An instinctive trust in the value of expediency and a complete absence of moral sense are the core of her personality, and both features are eminently relevant to the structure of the play. Expediency is a derisively irrelevant weapon against the destructive forces of passion, and Phèdre's love for Hippolyte cannot fluctuate according to circumstances. It is in vain that Œnone tries to persuade her that, since Thésée is dead, her love for Hippolyte has become a normal feeling; and again in vain that, when Thésée comes back, she implores her to forget her passion, now hopeless:

> Il faut d'un vain amour étouffer la pensée.　　(III, iii)

Expediency is not only irrelevant, it is also playing into the hands of the enemy, and it is through Œnone's scheme, intended to save Phèdre, that passion brings the destruction of Hippolyte and of Phèdre herself. The lack of moral sense in Œnone's outlook permeates her tactical moves but is also important in itself, as it opposes another destructive force: the feeling of moral guilt in Phèdre. Here also the opposition defeats its own purpose. Each of Œnone's most amoral statements:

> Votre flamme devient une flamme ordinaire,　　　(I, v)
>
> Il faut immoler tout, et même la vertu,　　　(III, iii)
>
> La faiblesse aux humains n'est que trop naturelle,　(IV, vi)

contains the promise of a new torture for Phèdre's guilty conscience until, too late, immorality is violently denounced and dismissed with a curse:

> Je ne t'écoute plus. Va-t'en, monstre exécrable.　(IV, vi)

After this, Œnone's part is over. Her suicide, reported to Thésée, is no personal tragedy but a logical and definitive exit.

One of the confidants deserves special mention, for he is one of Racine's most powerful creations: Narcisse. As confidant to both Néron and Britannicus, he takes an active part in the development of the action. One might be tempted to see him as a mere symbol of Néron's evil side, but although Narcisse never oversteps the limits of his dramatic function, the impact his personality makes on the audience is remarkable. The effect he produces is of unmitigated evil; every word he says provokes loathing and terror, as before a being belonging to another species.

I said in a previous chapter that one of the main reasons for the sympathy we feel for Racinian heroes is their transparency. What characterizes Narcisse is a feature which exists in all the confidants but which, in his case, assumes a particular effect: his opacity. In a very short soliloquy (II, viii) he mentions ruthless ambition as the motivation for his actions. This is less a brief glimpse at the workings of his inner self than a convenient way of labelling the character clearly through a straightforward statement, similar to the 'I am determined to be a villain' of Shakespeare's Richard III. For the rest of the time we watch in Narcisse the perfect technique of evil intelligence and nothing else. Néron and Britannicus are as transparent to him as they are to the audience, who can follow with horrified fascination every twist in his speeches with precise knowledge of how each of Narcisse's subtle tactical moves will work on Néron or Britannicus.

At the end of the play we are told by Burrhus that an expression of malignant joy reveals Narcisse's reaction to the murder of Britannicus. It is only then that evil in him manifests itself outwardly. Until that moment, throughout the tragedy, his face is expressionless. His tone is soft, gentle, quiet. There is no sign of emotion or feeling, no revelation of disappointment when he does not immediately succeed, no indication that he feels triumphant, not even a hint of cruelty. By turning once more to positive advantage the negative features of the confidant, Racine has given Narcisse a special personality which is tragically intensely effective; the cold serenity, deriving from opacity, is more sinister than any outburst of hatred.

It is right that, during the banquet, Narcisse's personality disintegrates in a sneer of triumphant glee: the opacity of the monster is now the privilege of Néron.

However tight the connection between action and character-ization, it does not account for all the facets of the heroes' personalities, nor is it sufficient to appreciate the full value of the dramatic action in the tragedy. Other relationships must be considered.

It is perhaps time now to look up and meet the invisible protagonists: the gods.

6

THE DOUBLE PATTERN:
TRAGEDY AND MORAL ORDER

It is not surprising to find the gods present in a tragedy. The first tragic heroes were, if not gods themselves, at least demigods. It is also part of the tradition that the superior forces destroying the hero should be closely linked with a supernatural power, the more terrifying in that its ways are mysterious and arbitrary.

The gods whom we find in the Racinian theatre are either the classical gods of Greece or Rome or, in the last two plays, the Jewish God of the Old Testament. The presence of this supernatural element, however traditional, in a kind of drama which excludes any irrelevant material, however precious, raises a number of questions as to its place and function. Does it affect the nature and significance of tragedy? Does it reveal in Racine's theatre the existence of a moral outlook, the suggestion of metaphysical problems? Is it related to the Christian religion? The problem has received a great deal of attention, particularly in the twentieth century, and the views of the critics show some degree of divergence.[1] The focusing of the present study on the organic cohesion of Racinian tragedy may, by precluding the interference of extraneous considerations, help us to place the Racinian gods according to their relevant function.

The first point to consider is their dramatic value in the structure of the tragedy, that is, the way in which they are used to increase the intensity of the tragic emotion without breaking the unity of the tragic pattern.

It must be noted immediately that there were severe limitations to the use Racine could make of the supernatural element.

---

[1] Some of these critical views will be mentioned in this chapter. For further consideration of the religious interpretations of Racine's tragedies, see the Appendix.

He had inherited the classical tradition and the pagan gods. The gods were already present in the subjects he borrowed from previous dramatists. But, although these gods and goddesses belonged to a beautiful and revered tradition, they had lost a great deal of their evocative and terrifying power by the second half of the seventeenth century. They had become literary conventions and were part of a poetic diction in which Neptune stood for the sea and Vénus for any pretty woman.

There was no question of giving back a spurious vitality to these deities by making them appear on the stage. The conventions of *vraisemblance* and *bienséances* could not tolerate any form of *merveilleux*: Vénus could not be conjured up before the audience to testify to her unimpaired sway over the world nor Jupiter descend from heaven in a flaming chariot to reaffirm his omnipotence. The interdiction of the *merveilleux chrétien* would equally have prevented Racine from introducing a miraculous, and therefore impressive, happening into his biblical tragedies.

However, these limitations need not be overstressed. As always with Racine, limitations and rules, far from being a hindrance, serve his artistic purpose.

It is obvious that, given the tightness of a Racinian tragedy, no miracle can be allowed to impede or modify in any way the impeccable working of the tragic mechanism. The dynamic structure of the play is, as we know, entirely dependent on the feelings of the characters. The actions of the gods do not interfere with this dramatic action because they coincide with it. In *Phèdre*, for instance, the human element, Phèdre's passion, and Vénus' decision to destroy her are completely fused. The heroine is at the same time the victim of her love and the victim of Vénus without the audience having the possibility of distinguishing between the two. The gods are thus assimilated to the destructive passions within the heart of man. Fate, which in past tragedies was an external power, takes in Racine the form of psychological determinism. The furies who drive

Oreste to madness come from his own self-torturing mind, and whatever the vagaries of their infernal chorus, their leader will always have the face of Hermione. The death of Hippolyte may appear to be the act of Neptune and the instrument of his death a mythical monster, but basically his fate is caused by the decisions taken by the nurse, Phèdre and Thésée; the latter could have sent a paid murderer to kill his son. The intervention of Neptune enhances the dramatic horror and has a poetic value but it does not alter the mechanism of psychological reactions which lead Hippolyte to his doom.

Some further remarks are perhaps needed in the case of *Iphigénie* and of *Athalie*. These are the two plays in which the divine element is very much in evidence. In *Iphigénie*, the gods twice impose—or seem to impose—their own decisions on the characters: first in asking Agamemnon to sacrifice his daughter; secondly, in revealing that Eriphile is the intended victim. The first intervention of the gods strikes us as a gratuitous move, external to human feelings. At this point it must be remembered that in a Racinian tragedy the mechanism of destruction has to be started by an external event. The interesting feature of *Iphigénie* is that the external event is of supernatural origin. We must also keep in mind the way in which Racine integrates this external event in the tragic pattern so that it soon appears as coming from the very nature of the heroes' passions. This is true of *Iphigénie* as of the other plays. The passion of ambition in Agamemnon is such that it must inevitably come into conflict with his strongest feelings. Clytemnestre's hatred for her husband is bound to provoke the most dangerous situation. Undoubtedly the cruel, even absurd, command of the gods strikes a note of capricious self-assertion; and yet its very unnaturalness seems to mirror the monstrous relations between Agamemnon and Clytemnestre. The fate of Eriphile, although it is explained by the decision of the gods, is at the same time the ineluctable result of her passions: she is as much destroyed

by her love for Achille and her jealousy of Iphigénie as by Calchas. It is significant that she rushes to the altar and kills herself
with her own hand.

In the case of *Athalie* one might be tempted to think that for
once the supernatural element, God, is the main cause of the
dramatic action, and some critics think so, even to the extent of
seeing in the characters mere puppets whose movements are
entirely directed by the will of God.[1] This is, I think, a very
questionable point of view and a somewhat crude simplification
of the play. I shall come back to the inaccuracy of this interpretation. But when we consider the dynamic pattern of *Athalie*
and leave aside, for the time being, the fact that the supernatural
element is here the Christian God, Racine's technique does not
appear to be different in this tragedy from what it is elsewhere.
As far as tragedy is concerned, God in *Athalie* plays the same
part as Vénus in *Phèdre*. Athalie is at the same time a victim of
God—

> Impitoyable Dieu, toi seul as tout conduit[2]   (v, vi)

—and of the terrible mechanism of frustrated ambition caused
by the decline of her power. Even the dangerous power of
attraction which the temple and the child have over her (and
incidentally on Mathan) and which causes her death is a human
reaction as well. Undeniably Joad asks God to instil in Athalie's
mind

> ...cet esprit d'imprudence et d'erreur,
> De la chute des rois funeste; avant-coureur   (i, ii)

but her tactical mistakes and rash decisions are nevertheless the
logical outcome of ambition and greed mixed with obsessive
memories of family crimes and a desperate wish to find peace
and put an end to the bloody saga of her dynasty.

This perfect fusion between the will of the gods and the

---

[1] 'Dans *Athalie*, Dieu est tout, et les différents moments de l'action ne sont pas
autre chose que les différents moments de sa pensée...' (Thierry Maulnier,
Racine, Paris, 1935, p. 300).

[2] Compare with Phèdre: C'est Vénus tout entière à sa proie attachée. (i, iii).

mechanism of human passions accounts for a most successful interplay of the two complementary elements.

On the one hand passion is given a supernatural enlargement which magnifies the hero and increases the intensity of the tragedy. This enlargement does not detract from the unity and coherence of the tragic pattern and is admirably relevant; for it is in keeping with the nature of passion that love, hatred, or ambition should appear as a kind of alien force within the heart of man, acting against man, in spite of man; and the terrifying power of this alien force is rightly emphasized by its assimilation to an all-powerful antagonistic supernatural being, Vénus or God.

On the other hand human passions give to the gods, especially to the pagan gods, the vitality they had lost in the course of the seventeenth century. Vénus had become a very powerless deity, with no more than an aura of dignity around her name; her fierce intimacy with Phèdre—

> C'est Vénus tout entière à sa proie attachée.

—brings back the goddess as a redoubtable, tangible reality:

> Je sentis tout mon corps et transir et brûler.
> Je reconnus Vénus et ses feux redoutables.   (I, iii)

It is through Phèdre's love and guilt that the classical myths recapture their evocative power. Lit up by her desperate wish to reach Hippolyte, the Cretan labyrinth reveals once more its treacherous paths, and one terrified glance upwards from her is enough for the sky to blaze with the presence of a hundred gods:

> ...et je soutiens la vue
> De ce sacré Soleil dont je suis descendue?
> J'ai pour aïeul le père et le maître des Dieux;
> Le ciel, tout l'univers est plein de mes aïeux.   (IV, vi)

If the gods are thus in Racine the accomplices in the destruction of man by his passions, it is not surprising that they should appear as possessing all the unfairness, arbitrary nature and cruelty of passion.

They certainly appear so to Oreste, and his relations with them assume the dramatic form of a progressive awareness on his part of their ruthlessness.

At the beginning of the play the gods of far-off barbaric lands, who insist on human sacrifices, are still remote:

> J'ai mendié la mort chez des peuples cruels
> Qui n'apaisaient leurs Dieux que du sang des mortels. (II, ii)

In the next act the evidence of their universal unfairness belongs to the hero's immediate surroundings:

> Je ne sais de tout temps quelle injuste puissance
> Laisse le crime en paix et poursuit l'innocence.
> De quelque part sur moi que je tourne les yeux,
> Je ne vois que malheurs qui condamnent les Dieux. (III, i)

He feels himself among those whose very innocence attracts the persecution of the gods and this feeling of helplessness provokes him to take the initiative and rush desperately ahead, challenging the gods to do their worst:

> Méritons leur courroux, justifions leur haine. (III, i)

The desperate urge to accede to his doom is matched by the desperate appraisal of his position when, at the end of the play, he turns to the gods who have answered his challenge beyond all expectations:

> Grâce aux Dieux! Mon malheur passe mon espérance:
> Oui, je te loue, ô Ciel, de ta persévérance.
> Appliqué sans relâche au soin de me punir,
> Au comble des douleurs tu m'as fait parvenir.
> Ta haine a pris plaisir à former ma misère:
> J'étais né pour servir d'exemple à ta colère,
> Pour être du malheur un modèle accompli. (v, v)

It remains for the gods to reveal their sinister presence beside Oreste: the hideous furies close about him and by then his hatred of the gods is such that his very last reaction is one of frenzied scorn; whatever tortures the messengers from heaven can devise, human beings can do still better:

> Mais non, retirez-vous, laissez faire Hermione:
> L'ingrate mieux que vous saura me déchirer;
> Et je lui porte enfin mon cœur à dévorer.   (v, v)

The gods do not protect the innocence of Hippolyte and dramatically ignore his faith in their justice:

> Sur l'équité des Dieux osons nous confier,

whereas they immediately answer the request of Thésée:

> Inexorables Dieux, qui m'avez trop servi!   (v, vi)

Thésée's final rejection of the gods reveals in him a kind of bitterness which goes deeper perhaps than Oreste's outbursts. Not only are the gods unfair, they are treacherous as well: their blessing is a curse in disguise, and those they befriend are the most wretched of all:

> Je hais jusques au soin dont m'honorent les Dieux;
> Et je m'en vais pleurer leurs faveurs meurtrières,
> Sans plus les fatiguer d'inutiles prières.
> Quoi qu'ils fissent pour moi, leur funeste bonté
> Ne me saurait payer de ce qu'ils m'ont ôté.   (v, vii)

In *Iphigénie*, the arbitrary commands of the gods, the shameful nature of their decisions, are openly acknowledged by Agamemnon: they can enforce their will but they cannot expect approval or respect:

> Ma fille, il est trop vrai. J'ignore pour quel crime
> La colère des Dieux demande une victime;
> Mais ils vous ont nommée...
> . . . . . .
> Faites rougir ces Dieux qui vous ont condamnée.   (IV, iv)

Eriphile refuses to give the gods the satisfaction of the ritual sacrifice. Her pride is more sacred to her than the sacred character of a religious ceremony:

Déjà pour la saisir Calchas lève le bras:
Arrête, a-t-elle dit, et ne m'approche pas.
Le sang de ces héros dont tu me fais descendre
Sans tes profanes mains saura bien se répandre.   (v, vi)

The part played by the gods or the heavens in the historical tragedies is, because of the subject, much more restricted. One could, however, find something like the arbitrariness of divine rules in the quality of taboo which the title of 'reine' has for Rome. It is also interesting to note that Néron considers that he has the gods on his side: they have not granted Octavie a child—
Les Dieux ne montrent point que sa vertu les touche
—and they would approve his love for Junie: (II, ii)

Les Dieux ont prononcé. Loin de leur contredire,
C'est à vous de passer du côté de l'Empire.   (II, iii)

In *Bajazet* the gods are absent, or at least blind and deaf. Atalide is the only character who expresses some faith in Heaven:

Il est vrai, si le ciel eût écouté mes vœux,
Qu'il pouvait m'accorder un trépas plus heureux;   (III, iv)

but at the end she takes upon herself alone the responsibility of the catastrophe.

It seems, therefore, that the gods in Racine do not represent any of the moral values one associates with the idea of a Christian God, such as justice and kindness, and, moreover, that the part they play is that of a literary device, a means of increasing the dramatic intensity of tragedy by the enlargement they provide, and a very effective way of underlining the fateful and cruel working of human passions. Fate is amoral, and fundamentally the tragic vision of Racine is outside Christianity and is limited to the world of nature and reason, like the vision of all the moralists.

★

Yet, for a long time now, critics have tried to connect Racine's tragic world with the Christian religion. We may feel suspicious of the arguments based on biographical data and may reject the influence of Port-Royal on Racine as a doubtful proof of the Jansenist outlook permeating his tragedies. But, during the past ten years or so the 'Jansenist' thesis has acquired a new vigour, partly because the sociological approach has pointed out the relevance of the religious context and mostly, I think, because there is a strong tendency in contemporary criticism to look for 'spiritual values' in any work of literature. The works of M. Lucien Goldmann[1] and of Professor Hubert[2] are characteristic of this metaphysical interpretation of Racine. Professor Hubert scarcely mentions biography and takes Racine's Jansenism for granted. His thesis is based on very subtle and persuasive analysis of some aspects and lines of the tragedies, and he sets out to prove that Racine's plays have a religious significance: Racine intends to show us that man cannot be saved by his own efforts, and the Racinian theatre is centred on the total vanity of man: vanity of perfection in *Bérénice*, vanity of liberty in *Bajazet*, vanity of glory in *Iphigénie*, or vanity of love in *Phèdre*. M. Goldmann's book is based on sociological criticism. His assumption is fundamentally very sound: a writer, he says, even if he is not clearly conscious of it, expresses a vision of man which corresponds to a social phenomenon—to wit, the views held by the community around him. Having selected Jansenism as the most important social phenomenon to be reflected in Racine's work, M. Goldmann endeavours to demonstrate that the dramatist's tragic vision is Jansenist, that is, the vision of a world where God is hidden; this world is necessarily wicked and the tragic hero is the man or woman who refuses the world, like Andromaque or Junie.

These two important works are well informed and intellectually attractive but they leave us, nevertheless, with the impression that the sociological arguments and the subtle

[1] *Le Dieu caché* (Paris, 1956). See also *Jean Racine, dramaturge* (Paris, 1956).
[2] *Essai d'exégèse racinienne—Les secrets témoins* (Paris, 1956).

exegeses are propped up against the Racinian text at a question-able angle. Moreover, other critics take a diametrically opposite view, and their refusal to acknowledge any Christian element in Racine goes extremely far. M. Michel Butor, sustaining his argument with illustrations of the cruelty and unfairness of the gods similar to those I have cited, does not hesitate to say that Racine's tragedies are marked by a hatred of the Divine and a thinly disguised taste for blasphemy.[1]

After such divergent views it is not surprising that we should be left wondering at the true significance of the supernatural element in the Racinian tragedies and that the gods, or God, in Racine should prove less tractable to a clear assessment than one might at first have thought.[2]

Conflicting views on the moral, even Christian, significance of Racine's tragedies may not, however, be impossible to re-concile. But, in order to attempt a reconciliation, it is imperative to distinguish very clearly between two different elements in the dramatic structure of a tragedy: the tragic pattern and the pattern of order.

The tragic pattern is what constitutes the tragedy proper and what I have been concerned with until this moment: the de-struction of the hero by superior forces. This tragic pattern has, in my opinion, no Christian significance, and it is right to con-sider that the gods, as we saw, may be used by Racine as a con-venient literary device to increase the intensity of the tragic emotion. The portrayal of the passions which destroy the hero may have its instructive side, as always with the moralists, since it contributes to our knowledge of man. But such a 'moral' value is not connected with any particular code of ethics. The spectator or the reader may feel disturbed by such intimations of

---

[1] 'Racine et les dieux', in *Répertoire* (Editions de Minuit, 1959).

[2] In fact the latest article devoted to the question of the gods in Racine, by Professor R. C. Knight ('Les Dieux païens dans la tragédie française', in *Revue d'histoire littéraire de la France*, juillet–septembre, 1964) ends on a note of interrogation.

the dangerous potentialities enclosed in the human heart; he is not, on the other hand, facing a revelation of man's metaphysical condition. The ultimate value of the tragic pattern belongs to the field of aesthetics and will be examined in the next chapter.

But there is another structural element in a tragedy, distinct from the tragic pattern. When I considered the main features of a tragedy in the first chapter of this book, I mentioned order. Whatever the scope of the tragic disaster, the unbearable suffering, and the nature of the final catastrophe, a tragedy does not, as a rule, leave the audience with the feeling that the world has come to an end. Life goes on, values remain; even if the individual hero is annihilated. In the most ancient prototype of tragedy of which we know, this basic need for a pattern of order transcending the individual fate of the tragic protagonist found its expression in the rebirth of the mythical hero after his destruction at the hands of superior powers. A pattern of order emerges from the Greek tragedies, at least at the end of each trilogy. In Shakespeare the last scene of even the darkest of his tragedies indicates the return of order: *Macbeth* ends with the welcome given to the new king of Scotland; even in *King Lear* —a play where the destructive forces of tragedy seem to be focused on the theme of chaos—after Lear dies desperate, Edgar stands up and assumes the task of shaping the future.

In a good tragedy, the indication of some kind of order, political, moral or religious, does not blunt the impact of the tragic pattern but provides it with a framework which is necessary to the comfort of the audience. Therefore, this pattern of order is in keeping with the values of the spectators and varies according to contemporary ideas on politics, ethics or religion. This is the point where the sociological approach can be a great help in enlightening us as to the kind of political or moral climate the dramatist at a given period would register in his pattern of order. Obviously Corneille or Racine, writing for a seventeenth-century audience, was bound to write within the framework of a certain conception of kingship and of Christian moral values. In the case of Racine, one would hesitate to relate Christian values too closely to Jansenism. If we leave aside the biographical approach (which ought to be irrelevant here, as the suggested order is that of the audience and not necessarily that of the playwright), the influence of Jansenist thought on the second half of the seventeenth century is so diffuse that it is difficult to assess.

Moral order in Racine is, of course, different from that in Corneille. Moreover, the use made by the dramatist of the pattern of order is not, in the case of a great dramatist, limited to a perfunctory gesture at the end of the play to reassure the audience, nor does it fulfil the same dramatic function in every play. In fact nothing is more revealing of Racine's flexibility in dramatic technique than the different relations between the two patterns—that of tragedy and that of order—to be found in his theatre.

Athalie gives us the clearest illustration of the double pattern. The tragic pattern is centred, as we have seen, on the destruction of Athalie by the superior power of God, who uses the queen's passions in order to defeat her. This superior power works against the heroine in the unfair, cruel and amoral way in which fate always works in a tragedy. Athalie is as much destroyed through her better feelings, such as her pity for the child Joas, as through her greed and ambition. Her undoing is, moreover, stamped with the supreme characteristic of tragedy: that of making us wonder at a sort of wanton gratuitousness on the part of fate, since the ruler who replaces her will be morally worse than she is. Therefore, we grant Athalie the kind of sympathy we feel towards the tragic hero. Her final outburst, her desperate cry of hatred and her challenge provoke in us a violent, heartfelt desire to side with her against Joas, Joad and God; and the echoes of her prophetic curse linger on, with sinister irony, in the hollowness of Joas' prayer:

Dieu, qui voyez mon trouble et mon affliction,
Détournez loin de moi sa malédiction,
Et ne souffrez jamais qu'elle soit accomplie.
Faites que Joas meure avant qu'il vous oublie.   (v, vii)

Parallel to the tragic pattern, the pattern of order runs throughout the play. It is the Christian order, in which the crowning of Joas makes sense because in a distant future the line of David will lead to Christ. The Christian order, that of the audience, is therefore projected back into the Jewish story as a framework to it. The Christian virtues of justice, charity and gentleness are repeatedly voiced by the chorus, by Josabet and at times by Joad. The last lines of the play, spoken by Joad, assert the solidity of the moral order:

Apprenez, roi des Juifs, et n'oubliez jamais
Que les rois dans le ciel ont un juge sévère,
L'innocence un vengeur, et l'orphelin un père.   (v, viii)

Even if the tragic pattern has resulted in replacing a criminal queen by an even more criminal king, and whatever the evil ways of individual kings, the concept of the good Christian ruler remains an unshaken value and divine justice shines on, untarnished, affixed on a Christian sky.

Any attentive reader is more or less conscious of this double pattern in *Athalie*, but Racinian criticism since Sainte-Beuve has tended to subordinate one pattern to the other and, as a rule, to give the Christian pattern such an overwhelming importance that it blurs the outlines of the tragic pattern.[1]

It seems to me that the two patterns are organized according to an extremely skilful parallelism. The parallelism was a necessity here. Given the subject, a brief reminder of the Christian order at the end of the play would have been insufficient, and therefore the pattern of order is constantly present during the course of the play. But Racine does not allow it to interfere with the intensity of the tragic pattern. Quite the contrary: it

[1] Cf. Thierry Maulnier's interpretation of the play, quoted above, p. 115, n. 1.

intensifies and enriches the tragic emotions felt by the audience. Athalie is the more to be pitied for being the individual sacrificed to the birth of Christianity and to an ideal of kingship which she could not possibly share. According to her own lights she has been an efficient non-Christian ruler:

> Sur d'éclatants succès ma puissance établie
> A fait jusqu'aux deux mers respecter Athalie.
> Par moi Jérusalem goûte un calme profond.   (II, v)

The peace she has established is founded on the respect and consideration which her strength and political judgment inspire among the neighbouring countries, and she is justified, as regards wordly politics, in speaking with some pride of her wisdom as a ruler. The double pattern gives Joad a double face, which opens up terrifying depths in the character. The sudden shifts from the inspired prophet to the cunning politician, from the violence of the bloodthirsty leader to the quiet serenity of God's elect—not merely shifts but also at times an inextricable blend of conflicting attitudes—add a sinister complexity to the dramatic movement of the play. This powerful ambiguity between fair and foul assumes supernatural proportions in the constant and disturbing ambiguity of God. In the tragic pattern God appears cruel, unfair and moved by an arbitrary wish to destroy Athalie. As such there exists between Him and Athalie the kind of intimacy which, in a tragedy, places the hero almost on a level with the superior power which defeats him. God pursues Athalie into the secret depths of her dreams. She unmasks Him at the end and acknowledges her defeat with an insulting tone of pride which appears justified, given the personal relations between the two opponents. At the same time, as we watch the terrifying duel, we are aware of the outlines of the pattern of order drawn on the backcloth. The stature of the heroine and our feeling of terror are magnified as we realize that the brutal and treacherous God who destroys Athalie and who is so dangerously near is also the God of order who stands for all justice and wisdom, far above the human tilt-yard, eternally serene and out of reach.

In *Iphigénie* also, the supernatural element is to be found both in the tragic pattern and in the pattern of order. But in this case there is no need to justify the ways of the pagan gods to the audience, and accordingly the gods appear as the gods of moral order only at the end of the play; they allow Iphigénie to escape death, they even agree to consider Eriphile's suicide as a suitable substitute for the barbaric procedure of ritual sacrifice. On the other hand, the frightening and destructive power of the gods is felt throughout the play and is overwhelmingly important in the tragic pattern. Not only are the gods responsible for starting the cruel mechanism of psychological determinism in Agamemnon, Eriphile and all the other characters, but we are constantly reminded also of their future ruthlessness towards all the protagonists: Achille's short span of life has been measured exactly by them, Ulysse's wanderings mapped by their will, and their curse on the descendants of Atreus and Thyestes has shaped the monstrous saga of the unfortunate family of Agamemnon.

Andromaque offers the interesting feature of a play in which the gods are related only to the tragic pattern; particularly in their persecution of Oreste. Moral order is not expressed in terms of supernatural elements. It is represented by Andromaque, and the pattern of order is delicately unobtrusive throughout the play, like that of a frieze carved in sunk relief, since the order Andromaque opposes to the tragic passion of the other characters, her moral integrity, is related to a dead hero and a dead city. Yet she and her son triumph at the end, order asserts itself positively then; this triumph coincides with poetic justice and fits in with the pattern of rebirth after destruction which is the basic pattern of order in tragedy. It is the revenge of Troy, the Greeks having destroyed themselves through their own passions.

Andromaque's triumph is a political victory, Junie's a moral one. Moral order is restored at the end of *Britannicus* when the Roman people kill Narcisse—that superb creation of pure evil—and when the House of the Vestals offers Junie permanent protection. This moral order does not detract in any way from the intense dramatic value of the tragic pattern centred on Néron and Agrippine. As, in *Andromaque*, it is Pyrrhus' tragic fate to love a woman who stands for a poetic justice which condemns him, so it is part of the destructive working of passion in Néron that the object of his love should be Junie. More subtle than Pyrrhus, who misses the point of poetic justice ('Brûlé de plus de feux que je n'en allumai'), Néron is aware of that particular moral quality in Junie and is both attracted and irritated by it:

> Et c'est cette vertu, si nouvelle à la cour,
> Dont la persévérance irrite mon amour;   (II, ii)

and he desperately wishes to possess and suppress it. Junie escapes him for ever, so that the final restoration of moral order increases the hopelessness of Agrippine's and Néron's individual fates and brings into particular relief the tragic implications contained in the last sentence of the play, spoken by Burrhus:

> Plût aux Dieux que ce fût le dernier de ses crimes!

Nowhere perhaps is the final triumph of order more conspicuous than in *Mithridate*, so much so that one critic considers it the least tragic of Racine's plays.[1] This judgment, however, needs some slight rectification. It is true that the play ends with the restoration of moral order: the treacherous Pharnace has fled and will receive his punishment, mutual love is rewarded, Xipharès has atoned for his mother's past treason, Mithridate dies with dignified grandeur made more peaceful and impressive by his final generosity. Moreover, the audience is left with the intimation of the future defeat of Rome. Rome, which in the play stands for tyranny, will meet her fate in the very

---

[1] R. Picard, Introduction to *Mithridate*, in *Œuvres complètes de Racine*, p. 595.

way that Mithridate had foreseen when revealing to his sons his last magnificent plan against his enemy:

Jamais on ne vaincra les Romains que dans Rome.   (III, i)

Yet the tragic pattern remains, the more tragic perhaps as it is precisely the exquisite moral code of Xipharès and Monime that has brought not only suffering to themselves but the destruction of Mithridate also. There is throughout the play a tragic contrast between the overwhelming pride and brutal strength of Mithridate and the delicate and scrupulous attitude of Xipharès and Monime, the deceptively fragile nature of their love; and the lethal power of love is perhaps the stronger when, as in Monime, the ever-present violence of absolute passion is controlled by fastidious rules of moral dignity.

The two tragedies which are the most interesting and the most successful, I think, from the point of view of the double pattern, are *Bérénice* and *Phèdre* because, in these two plays, the tragic pattern and the pattern of order are connected very closely and even fused at times.

Moral and political order is at the very centre of Titus' inner struggle, and he knows that such an order implies the destruction of himself as an individual. It is, of course, very much in keeping with the arbitrary and essentially amoral working of fate in the tragic pattern that the hero should be destroyed through his crimes or through his virtues, indifferently. Titus and Bérénice are destroyed by making the choice of accepting moral order. Their final separation will be, as we know, the worst form of inner destruction, since they will have to live with the torture of undiminished passion and the added torments for Bérénice of being at last totally assured of Titus' love:

Je connais mon erreur, et vous m'aimez toujours.   (v, vii)

The end of the play achieves a magnificent fusion of the two patterns, the more successful as they remain, through an almost miraculous balance, perfectly distinct. On this point I strongly disagree with Professor Hubert who sees in the final generosity of the three characters a kind of theatrical and useless striving after perfection.[1] This to me, although Professor Hubert stresses the difference between Corneille and Racine, would imply, nevertheless, that Titus, Bérénice and Antiochus experience a moment of proud exaltation of the kind which we associate with the Cornelian hero. There is, I think, no expression of *personal* glory in the scene. The order which triumphs benefits Rome and the universe; it does not transcend or alter the passions of the characters. Undoubtedly it is an impressive triumph, nobly acknowledged by the protagonists. At the same time, the tragic pattern stands out in implacable outline; the triumph of order coincides with the annihilation of the heroes. Unlike Auguste, Bérénice does not ask the universe and future generations to remember the exalted moment of a sublime victory, but only the infinite misery of their individual destinies:

> Adieu: servons tous trois d'exemple à l'univers
> De l'amour la plus tendre et la plus malheureuse
> Dont il puisse garder l'histoire douloureuse.   (v, vii)

The extreme beauty of this scene lies in giving us at the same time, through the same words, the impersonal nobility of restored order and the tragic price paid for it. Antiochus' 'Hélas!' seals the complete destruction of those human beings that were Titus, Bérénice and himself. Nothing is left but their public image, rigidly enthroned at the appointed places in the political order.

Phèdre also ends with the triumph of moral order, with Thésée's repentance and his reconciliation with Aricie. But it is in Phèdre herself that the connection between the pattern of order and the tragic pattern is particularly remarkable.

[1] 'Titus, en renonçant à la vie afin de préserver aux yeux de sa maîtresse et de tout l'univers la perfection de son image impériale, est bien obligé de devenir semblable à un acteur qu'on applaudit. Et l'on sent que pour un janséniste aussi intransigeant que Racine, ce renoncement quelque peu théâtral et cependant humain est inutile et prend même une valeur ironique' (*Essai d'exégèse racinienne*, p. 139).

Everybody has noticed that Racine, on this point following Seneca and not Garnier, has given Phèdre a strong moral awareness of her guilt. Phèdre considers herself as outside a moral order which she acknowledges all the time. This worsens her tragic predicament. To the frustration typical of the Racinian setting for the destructive mechanism of passion is added another destructive element: the sense of guilt which accompanies her love and all its manifestations. In her the pattern of moral order itself becomes an element of the tragic pattern, as in the case of Titus, but with some differences. Titus may reproach himself for his delay and hesitations in accepting political order—

> Depuis huit jours je règne; et jusques à ce jour,
> Qu'ai-je fait pour l'honneur? J'ai tout fait pour l'amour.
> D'un temps si précieux quel compte puis-je rendre?   (IV, iv)

—but he never experiences the self-loathing, the constant and bitter confession of shame, the frenzied reactions of the hunted, the desperate search for the impossible hiding-place away from light, away from both heaven and hell, which her consciousness of moral order imposes on Phèdre.

Her last speech is one of the best examples of the perfect harmony which characterizes the tragic pattern in Racine. It ends with the mention of daylight, a key image in the play, which is used here to express Phèdre's destruction and also to underline once more the hopelessness of her love. Daylight is forever denied her, that is, not only life but also the object of her love, that transparent and adorable innocence, Hippolyte. The lines which bring together, in a most harrowing climax, the central elements of the tragic pattern are, at the same time, the lines which state the restoration of order. This is done with the greatest economy and therefore the most powerful effect, for it is the same image, that of the serenity of the pure light of day, which symbolizes the triumph of moral order:

Déjà je ne vois plus qu'à travers un nuage
Et le ciel, et l'époux que ma présence outrage;
Et la mort, à mes yeux dérobant la clarté,
Rend au jour, qu'ils souillaient, toute sa pureté.   (v, vii)

Here again, as at the end of *Bérénice*, the two patterns are perceived simultaneously and yet as distinct from each other. But in *Phèdre* the subtle and beautiful image which unites them gives to our tragic emotions and to the aesthetic catharsis we experience the greatest possible scope during that supreme moment when our image of Phèdre, our feelings, and even moral order, expand and dissolve in the transparent luminescence of a boundless sky.

There are two tragedies in which the relationship between order and the tragic raises special problems. One is *Esther*. The play is largely outside the scope of this study, as the word tragedy scarcely applies here and one may agree with most critics in viewing it as a kind of religious poem, of *opéra sacré*. But it is interesting to note at this point that *Esther* represents a case where the pattern of order supersedes the tragic pattern completely. This is done deliberately by Racine, and all the resources of his dramatic lyricism and of his stagecraft are directed towards the glorification of the Christian order. The difference in the use made of the chorus in *Athalie* and in *Esther* is significant. In both tragedies the chorus expresses the themes of Christian order. But in *Athalie* the chorus stands apart from the protagonists,[1] whereas in *Esther*, where the presence of Christian order permeates every scene, the chorus takes an active part in the dramatic pattern: gathering affectionately and symbolically round Esther (i, ii) or expressing personal reactions to the sight of Aman (iii, iii).

The other play in which we find an unorthodox use of the double pattern is *Bajazet*. It is a play which has always worried the critics and at times the audience (even when it was first

[1] See p. 92.

performed). I wonder whether the real cause for the uneasiness we feel does not lie in the rather strange use made by Racine of the pattern of order.

Critics have noticed the absence of the gods. Professor Vinaver has stressed that the play, by its very subject, is cut off from Western tradition and that the author could not have a gentleman's agreement with his audience as to the ultimate significance of the play.[1] The point is important and closely related to the problem which interests me.

It is true that we do not find in *Bajazet* a moral order which can satisfy the audience. In fact there is no transcendental moral order in the play. But there is order, the kind of order very rightly underlined and very well analysed by Professor Hubert:[2] the order mentioned by Roxane:

> Vous pouvez retourner, je n'ai rien à vous dire.
> Du sultan Amurat je reconnais l'empire.
> Sortez. Que le Sérail soit désormais fermé,
> Et que tout rentre ici dans l'order accoutumé.   (II, ii)

'L'ordre accoutumé' is the order established by the sultan Amurat. This invisible character represents order and it is round him that the pattern of order is woven. His messengers constantly remind us and the characters that the will and decisions of the sultan stand for the stability of the country. From the beginning it is obvious that order has been upset:

> OSMIN Et depuis quand, Seigneur, entre-t-on dans ces lieux,
> Dont l'accès était même interdit à nos yeux?
> Jadis une mort prompte eût suivi cette audace;   (I, i)

and all the characters, at the end, will pay the penalty of their revolt against Amurat.

It is the only order. If at times Bajazet and Atalide give the impression that their feelings coincide with some moral ideal of courage or integrity, such reactions on their part are not

---

[1] *Racine and Poetic Tragedy*, trans. P. Mansell Jones (Manchester University Press, 1955), pp. 41–44.
[2] *Essai d'exégèse racinienne*, ch. VII, particularly pp. 143–147.

moral reactions.[1] They are simply in keeping with the stylized mechanism of passion, as always in Racine. Passion in the absolute does not admit of any compromise and therefore Bajazet cannot possibly pretend that he loves Roxane.

The interesting point in *Bajazet* is that the order is a wicked order, that it is based on slavery and goes against the conception of order of a seventeenth-century audience (or a twentieth-century one). At the same time this order is so powerful that even the dream of fighting enslavement is impossible and when Atalide, before dying, conjures up past heroes:

> Vous, de qui j'ai troublé la gloire et le repos,
> Héros, qui deviez tous revivre en ce héros,   (v, xii)

it is only to stress the annihilation of all possible hope in a better world.

The particular nature of the pattern of order affects the whole play. What happens in *Bajazet* is exactly the reverse of what happens in *Esther*. The tragic pattern supersedes the pattern of order entirely. We saw how the two patterns blend in Phèdre herself. In *Bajazet*, too, order becomes a destructive force, and that in all the characters. But, whereas the moral order which contributes to the destruction of Phèdre retains its value and is unquestioningly accepted by the audience, in *Bajazet* the order which destroys all the protagonists partakes of the same arbitrary, amoral and cruel character as passion and fate. Hence the alarming negativeness of the framework in this tragedy: *Bajazet* takes place in Hell.

It is undoubtedly a departure from the general structure of traditional tragedy. We find a similar departure from dramatic orthodoxy in Molière's *Dom Juan*. In a comedy the gentlemen's agreement between the playwright and the audience, when it is explicit, rests on the *raisonneur*, whose task it is to voice the

---

[1] Here again I disagree with Professor Hubert, who sees a definite moral heroism in Bajazet and, to a lesser degree, in Atalide (*Essai d'exégèse racinienne*, pp. 146–159).

normal attitude of the spectators towards the subject of the play. As such, he gives them a standpoint from which to appreciate the comic distortion, and also the assurance that their moral or social values are safe. Therefore the *raisonneur's* part in the comic pattern can only be that of a foil. If his function of representing social order gets lost in the comic pattern, the audience is left without a norm, without a pattern of order, which is what happens in the case of Sganarelle and partly accounts for the feelings of uneasiness produced in the reader or the spectator. Perhaps both Racine and Molière were hampered by the subjects of their plays. Racine certainly insists in his preface on the particular atmosphere of 'férocité' of the Turkish story. However, the comparison between Molière and Racine should not be carried too far. The semi-failure of *Dom Juan* has other causes than the *raisonneur bafoué*. I wanted only to show the risk taken by the dramatist when he alters the function of the pattern of order. *Bajazet* remains a superb play, perhaps the most harrowingly tragic in the theatre of Racine (the lack of a moral background increasing the terrifying feeling of claustrophobia) and is certainly his boldest experiment.

★

It seems therefore that a reconciliation between two opposite views on Racine is possible. Contemporary moral values, even Christian values, are relevant to Racine's tragedies since they are taken into consideration in the pattern of order. They do not alter, however, the fundamentally amoral and timeless essence of the tragic.

And yet there have been discussions in the past as to the moral value of the tragic pattern itself and these discussions have centred round a definition of catharsis. They may have been no more than an effort to justify the existence of a literary genre; or perhaps an attempt to assess its ultimate value, which, in one way or another, is of necessity the final goal of any criticism.

7

THE AESTHETIC CATHARSIS

Catharsis is a very obscure notion and the efforts to interpret it in the course of centuries have made it even more obscure. The starting-point was a brief statement in Aristotle according to which tragedy, through inspiring pity and terror, purges these emotions. I do not propose to go through the various interpretations of this sentence. One interpretation, however, must be mentioned, as it held some credit in the minds of some theorists in the sixteenth and seventeenth centuries and even lingered on afterwards: the beneficial effect of purgation was extended to all passions and therefore tragedy was considered as having a moral action on the audience in providing an outlet for their passions, that is, their bad instincts, and also in enabling them to see clearly the deplorable results of unchecked feelings. But even in the seventeenth century this view was not unchallenged. Corneille stated that, in his opinion, this kind of utilitarian value of tragedy was purely imaginary. However, the best attack on catharsis and the would-be moral value of tragedy was launched by Bossuet in his *Maximes sur la Comédie*. The demonstration is remarkable, based on a very acute analysis of the effects on the spectators of a good tragedy. A bad tragedy, of course, says Bossuet, can be moral, or, more exactly, a moral tragedy is necessarily bad artistically. For him successful tragedies—he was obviously thinking of tragedies like those of Racine (which he admired as works of art and disapproved of on religious grounds)—tend to awake our passions. We are in sympathy with the characters who experience them, the tragic heroes are presented to us as noble and attractive types of humanity, and the passions are made to appear beautiful through the art of the dramatist. There is very little to add to Bossuet's argument. The problem of the moral value of a Racinian tragedy is the same problem as is found in the case of all the seventeenth-century classicists, and the answer is the same. First, the classicist does not go against the established moral values of his time: he takes them for granted, and Racine's respect for them is shown in his careful delineation of the pattern of order. Secondly, if there is a positive moral value in the classicist's works, this value is the value of clear sightedness, which is not necessarily a Christian value. Racine's tragedies, like La Rouchefocauld's *Maximes* or La Fontaine's *Fables*, give us a lucid vision of man. But at this point we are very far from the moral effect of catharsis.

There is, however, a form of catharsis in Racine. It is not moral but intellectual or, more exactly, aesthetic. To his translation of Aristotle's famous sentence on catharsis Racine added a significant note: tragedy, by provoking these emotions (pity and fear), liberates them from excesses and 'les ramène à un état conforme à la raison'. This is precisely what we saw when studying the stylization of passions in Racinian tragedy and we notice at the same time that the logical pattern imposed on the violent movements of human passions, while satisfying us intellectually, paradoxically intensifies and illuminates our emotions. Therefore pity and terror are transformed into a very particular experience. Bossuet was right in asserting that the pattern chosen by the dramatist is concerned with art and not with a moral purpose. The ultimate value of the tragic pattern lies in a kind of aesthetic catharsis: the satisfaction of watching the most disruptive emotions being organized into a rational pattern which connects, blends and sets off all the components of the tragic story, including the slightest details, down to the almost imperceptible nuance of a word or the half-revealed twitch on the face of a character.

The aesthetic satisfaction is the greater in that the pattern unfolds in a special kind of atmosphere, deliberately cut off from ordinary life. When I considered the basic elements of tragedy at the beginning of this book, I mentioned ceremony and ritual. From its religious origin tragedy has kept a special quality of dignity, an atmosphere of solemnity. The climate of tragedy is that of the great problems of man's destiny. Therefore the aesthetic emotion includes feelings of exaltation and of communion with a heightened picture of the human condition. Hence the importance of the formal aspect of tragedy, suggesting the strict observance of ritual gestures, the pomp and majesty of public ceremonies.

In his preface to *Bérénice* Racine specifically mentions this particular quality of the aesthetic emotion which must be felt by the audience watching a tragedy:

Ce n'est point une nécessité qu'il y ait du sang et des morts dans une tragédie: il suffit que l'action en soit grande, que les acteurs en soient heroïques, que les passions y soient excitées, et que tout s'y ressente de cette tristesse majestueuse qui fait tout le plaisir de la tragédie.

The effect of majesty in Racine is partly derived from elements which I have already examined, such as the choice of subject and characters. The well-known plots are part of the cultural heritage of the audience and as such possess the traditional value we associate with religious ceremony. Even the fact that the story holds no surprise for the spectators fits admirably with the ritualistic nature of tragedy. The men and women who attend mass in a Catholic church know beforehand the succession of steps leading to the sacrifice.

The protagonists in Racine's tragedies are, as we know, removed from our everyday existence, not only because of their high rank, but also because they belong to a world of history or legend. As such they are larger and nobler than ordinary human beings. Ageless through having lived so long in literary works, they are part of an aristocracy born of our Western culture; they have thus been chosen as a magnified representation of man, and we must consider them in a different way from the way in which we would look at real men and women.

Les personnages tragiques doivent être regardés d'un autre œil que nous ne regardons d'ordinaire ceux que nous avons vus de si près.

(Préface to *Bajazet*)

The first means of making the tragic characters appear different from people we are used to seeing, as well as of increasing the solemnity of the representation, is to rely on visual effects. In ancient Greece actors wore mask and cothurnus. In the seventeenth century they were dressed splendidly in contemporary costumes; thus were stressed two elements of the visual effect: the negation of realism and the importance of magnificence. In a modern performance of Racine costumes may vary; the only things which matter are that they should be stylized so as not to suggest any realistic reconstruction of a period and that they should be beautiful.

In the same way acting was highly stylized in the seventeenth century. There were conventions: definite gestures symbolizing a movement of surprise, an attitude of supplication or of despair. Obviously in a twentieth-century production some form of dignified stylization must be retained.[1]

But the formal dignity of Racinian tragedy does not rely basically on the visual element. All that is required from the latter is rather a negative quality: that it should be unobtrusive, except for a general impression of ceremonious magnificence. The positive dignity is to be found elsewhere.

This first appears in the very structure of the play, the simplicity of which has often been compared to the majestic simplicity of classical architecture. The simple and noble outline of a Greek column is the result of mathematical calculation, and the same is true of the architecture of a Racinian tragedy. Critics have noticed that Andromaque's tears or the tears of Bérénice are placed mathematically at the very centre of the play. The return of Thésée also occurs exactly in the middle of

---

[1] Unfortunately it happens only too often that we see Hermione shrugging her shoulders like a fishwife, Athalie gesticulating like an irate Marseillaise, and a fidgety Néron restlessly pacing the stage.

Phèdre. I have already mentioned that Phèdre's first and last lines represent in a way two identical moments. As in the case of Greek temple, we are not aware of all the calculations unless we start looking very closely and counting the lines, but we are conscious of an overall effect of symmetry and harmony.

On the other hand, there is another element of formal dignity that is easily perceived: the civility which marks the relationships between the characters and which is constantly underlined by the ceremonious form of address: Seigneur, Madame. As we know, the formality of this etiquette increases the dramatic intensity of frustration in the characters, being one more barrier between them. At the same time it increases the effect of dignity. The magnifying of man is here in keeping with the supreme elegance of manners of a refined civilization. Other conventions of classical drama which contribute to intensifying the tragic predicament of the characters—such as the absence of physical violence and the discarding of physical relationships between lovers—contribute also to the dignity of the civilized man, magnified through the very sophistication of his tastes and manners.

There remains the most important aspect of the ritualistic element in Racine, what Thierry Maulnier has rightly called 'la royauté du langage'. As this critic remarks,[1] language reigns supreme in Racine and is the only means of communicating emotion. No *décor*, no music (with the exception of the lyrics of the chorus), no song, no dance. The actor speaks, listens, or is silent. Language is everything. And what is meant by language is not any sound produced by the human mouth, but articulate language, a clear intellectual means of communication. We do not find any of those instinctive utterances which some other dramatists use to convey emotion: no shrieks, no shouting, not a groan of pain.

[1] It is a pleasure to mention here the two chapters which Thierry Maulnier has devoted to the language of Racine: 'La Royauté du langage', pp. 74–88, and 'Poésie impure', pp. 155–181, in *Racine*.

This language is a poetic language and no assessment of Racine's perfection can be complete unless one realizes the perfect fusion in him of the poet and the dramatist.

★

To appreciate the poetry of Racine requires a certain effort, and not only on the part of the English reader who might be tempted to compare it with Shakespeare's very different kind of dramatic poetry; even a French twentieth-century reader finds it difficult to face a kind of poetic language which goes against all his *idées reçues* on what is poetic and what is not; so much so that a number of contemporary critics have done their best to make the poetic world of Racine fit in with a conception of poetry which our century has inherited from Romanticism.[1]

Nevertheless, it is much more rewarding to appreciate Racine's poetic achievement in the light of seventeenth-century aesthetics, not only because any other approach is anachronistic but also because it is probably the only interpretation which reveals the absolute coherence of a Racinian tragedy.

Conventions and limitations are the essence of French classicism. Racine did not revolt against the limitations imposed on his poetic medium—limitations on vocabulary, on images—any more than he did against the dramatic conventions. As with the unities or the *bienséances*, he turned the prescribed limitations into advantages, even to the extent of making us wonder whether they are not at the very centre of his success.

The first thing to notice is the neutral quality of the poetic instrument used by Racine, whether we consider the alexandrine or the shorter metres to be found in the non-dramatic religious poems and in the choruses of *Esther* and *Athalie*. This instrument Racine inherited from Malherbe and its essential claim to perfection was that no confusion with prose was

[1] These trends in modern criticism will be mentioned in the Appendix.

possible. The aesthetic triumph of Malherbe had been to create a fastidious structural pattern inside the line and inside a poem, which set off the subtle melody of French sonorities. The same fastidiousness accounted for the purity of diction, the use of images which were acknowledged by a respected tradition, and a rhetoric equally supported by letters patent of nobility. Prosody and rhetoric combined in the most exquisite way so that the verse could be either vigorously rhythmical or elegantly fluid. The Malherbian ideal was thus concerned primarily with the purely aesthetic satisfaction of finding a beautiful form in exact harmony with the content of a poem. We are told that he considered poetry as a sort of dance in which graceful movements were guided by reason.

After Malherbe, and particularly in the second half of the century, the impression given by French poetry is that Malherbe's superb achievement had not greatly benefited any poet, and there was a striking contrast between the perfection of the poetic instrument and the poverty of poetic themes. This state of things was very clearly noticed and registered by some contemporary critics, particularly by Père Rapin in his *Réflexions sur la Poétique d'Aristote et sur les Ouvrages des Poètes anciens et modernes*, published in 1674. He is certainly very appreciative of the elegance and refinement which versification and poetic style have reached in his century. He knows what subtle uses the poet can make of words, including certain types of ambiguities. But at the same time he deplores the fact that in his age the poet's art seems limited to form only and concludes sadly, 'La grande poésie n'est pas en usage parmi nous.'

These remarks may well come back to our minds when we read Racine's non-dramatic works. I shall not mention his early poems, as it would be too easy and unfair to show how the poetic content which was to be found in former poets, such as Théophile de Viau and even Malherbe himself, has vanished. On the other hand, Racine's religious lyrics cannot fail to delight any reader who knows the value not only of the most delicate harmonies but also of an impeccable concord between style and themes. The themes are impersonal religious feelings within the biblical and Christian tradition. The choice of words, their evocative power, as well as the tone of the poem, are exactly limited to the tenor of restrained religious fervour. The result is a truly Malherbian perfection, poetry as a dance, which is here a sacred and graceful dance in honour of a collective religious belief. This dance, almost gratuitously beautiful in Racine's *Hymnes* and *Cantiques spirituels*, appears also in the choruses of the biblical tragedies but finds there a definite function which completes its purely aesthetic value.

Another classical poet, La Fontaine, overcame the difficulties inherent in this crisis of French poetry mentioned by Père Rapin and created a masterpiece in the field of non-dramatic poetry. In the case of Racine, however, it was left to tragedy to reveal the great poet. His tragic world gave to the aesthetic ideal an emotional content which is infinitely rich and, moreover, the only possible reality which could be expressed poetically without violating in any way the principles that sustained this ideal. All the resources of Malherbe's poetics, vigour and fluidity of the verse, limitations on diction, unobtrusiveness of imagery, seem to have been created out of all eternity to find their uses in the Racinian tragedy.

This tragedy requires its own atmosphere. We have seen that Malherbe's main concern was to operate a radical separation between prose and poetry. In fact the beauty, even, paradoxically, the solidity, of the great poetic architectural creations in Malherbe or his disciples came from the fact that they did not touch the ground at any point. Racinian tragedy, from the start, sets an impassable barrier between ordinary language and the language of the characters. Of course poetic drama is always based on the convention that the characters speak a different language from that of everyday life, and this establishes some kind of distance between the characters and ourselves. But in the case of some dramatists, such as Shakespeare, the distance varies with the variety of styles introduced, from blank verse to stylized prose. In Racine the distance is invariable. All the characters speak the same language. Giraudoux was wrong to complain that some of the lines he liked best in Racine, such as

Mais tout dort, et l'armée, et les vents, et Neptune,

(*Iphigénie*, I, i)

were spoken by confidants. The confidants' speeches are part of the same homogeneous poetic substance as the speeches spoken by the main protagonists. This evenness of texture is one of the major qualities of the Racinian poetic universe and I shall come back to it. The constant level of poetic speech emphasizes the distance between our ordinary world—the world of approximate, often shapeless or discordant, language—and the dignified, supremely logical world of tragedy. With the first line of a Racinian tragedy we enter a kind of sphere. The poetic substance which constitutes its rarefied atmosphere is the only one the characters and the audience can breathe in. One word out of tune, a single paragraph in prose, would shatter the crystal of the sphere.

The simplicity and naturalness of certain sentences in Racine should not deceive us into thinking that, as has sometimes been said, 'Racine rase la prose'. Those sentences that seem to have been taken straight from prosaic, ordinary language—'Bajazet, écoutez, je sens que je vous aime', or the famous 'Qui te l'a dit?', 'Sortez'—are woven into a stylistic and prosodic web which alters considerably their intrinsic value and confers upon them the dignity of a *langage à part*. The function, even the necessity, of occasional simplicity in diction and construction was considered by Père Rapin to be an essential part of the poet's craft: 'Il y a une rhétorique particulière à la poésie...qui consiste à savoir bien précisément et ce qu'il faut dire figurément, et ce qu'il faut dire tout simplement.' This quality of naturalness will be mentioned again, as well as its particular function in Racine's poetry.

So far we are still, so to speak, at the surface of the sphere, concerned only with the formal framework of the Racinian poetic universe. There remains the essential problem, to see how, inside the perfect alexandrines, the words which express the tragic situation become poetry.

The answer is in keeping with all we have seen of Racine's art up to now. The poetic value of a Racinian line is the result of a centripetal movement. It is the concentration and focusing of different elements, each one not necessarily poetic in itself, which gives to the verse its poetic quality.

Moreover, the focal point where all these elements meet to give an intense value to a word or a sentence, infinitely removed from its ordinary connotation, coincides exactly with the maximum dramatic intensity the word or the line conveys in the tragic pattern.

It is now that the modern reader has to struggle against certain preconceptions. In the twentieth century we believe only too easily that the beauty of a line or of an image transcends its context. We also tend to measure the perfection of poetry in relation to its power of expansion and to associate the poetic emotion with a kind of ecstasy which opens up infinite vistas.

The poetic universe of Racine is not concerned with expansion but with depth. It is a closed world in which the evocative power of a word, of an image, of a musical sonority, exists only within a complex network of relations and only through those relations.

Such poetry seems to challenge analysis, for how is one to cut into a closely knit pattern which includes the whole tragedy and all its aspects? Besides, given the internal coherence of a Racinian tragedy, the evenness of texture of the poetic medium, and the perfect fusion between the dramatic and poetic elements, it follows that all the lines are equally poetic and the choice of an illustration can only be arbitrary or dictated by subjective reasons.

But, although no analysis can be complete, one may at least consider some of the relations which give to Racine's poetry its individual value.

The most obvious is the one which connects the dramatic importance of a line and its poetic beauty. Undoubtedly the most striking feature of Racine's poetry in his tragedies is that it is strictly functional. This, incidentally, conforms to one of the cardinal principles of the Malherbian ideal: the perfect connection between content and form.

As an illustration I take the passage in which Néron describes to Narcisse how he fell in love with Junie, because for a newcomer to Racine the poetic achievement is here perhaps easier to perceive than elsewhere:

> Excité d'un désir curieux,
> Cette nuit je l'ai vue arriver en ces lieux,
> Triste, levant au ciel ses yeux mouillés de larmes,
> Qui brillaient au travers des flambeaux et des armes:
> Belle, sans ornements, dans le simple appareil
> D'une beauté qu'on vient d'arracher au sommeil.
> Que veux-tu? Je ne sais si cette négligence,
> Les ombres, les flambeaux, les cris et le silence,
> Et le farouche aspect des ses fiers ravisseurs
> Relevaient de ses yeux les timides douceurs.
> Quoi qu'il en soit, ravi d'une si belle vue,
> J'ai voulu lui parler, et ma voix s'est perdue:
> Immobile, saisi d'un long étonnement,
> Je l'ai laissé passer dans son appartement.
> J'ai passé dans le mien. C'est là que solitaire,
> De son image en vain j'ai voulu me distraire:
> Trop présente à mes yeux, je croyais lui parler;
> J'aimais jusqu'à ses pleurs que je faisais couler.
> Quelquefois, mais trop tard, je lui demandais grâce;
> J'employais les soupirs, et même la menace.

Voilà comme, occupé de mon nouvel amour,
Mes yeux, sans se fermer, ont attendu le jour.
Mais je m'en fais peut-être une trop belle image;
Elle m'est apparue avec trop d'avantage:
Narcisse, qu'en dis-tu?   (ii, ii)

The picture conjured up by Néron has sometimes been compared to a Rembrandt. It stimulates and pleases our imagination by its contrasts: antithesis between the girl and the soldiers, between shade and light, shouts and silence, so that our attention tends to linger on the line:

Les ombres, les flambeaux, les cris et le silence.

But, as Thierry Maulnier has very rightly observed,[1] this is not Racine painting a poetic picture, it is Néron; and every detail of this chiaroscuro is relevant to Néron's passion, and to the place of Junie in the dramatic pattern of the play. There is in the way in which Néron expresses himself a complete and complex revelation of himself and of his love: the sadistic satisfaction in the brutality suggested by the antithesis 'farouche aspect'/'timides douceurs'; the mixture of irritation and attraction which Junie's innocence ('levant au ciel ses yeux', 'sans ornement', 'dans le simple appareil') causes in him; a faint hope that he has perhaps fallen in love with the aesthetic flavour of the scene and not with Junie herself; hence the deprecatory 'Que veux-tu? je ne sais si cette négligence...' and later 'Mais je m'en fais peut-être une trop belle image'.

At the same time the lines

J'ai voulu lui parler et ma voix s'est perdue;
Immobile, saisi d'un long étonnement,
Je l'ai laissé passer dans son appartement,

which mark a slight modification in rhythm and sonorities in the development of the speech, slowing down the pace and expressing an emotion of muted wonder, indicate the depth

[1] *Racine*, p. 173.

146

and genuine quality of Néron's passion. The basic and tragic complexity of this passion is magnificently rendered by the ambiguity of the line

J'aimais jusqu'à ses pleurs que je faisais couler,

implying that his love is such as to include everything in Junie, even her tears, but also suggesting in him a somewhat sadistic satisfaction in recalling those tears.

The analysis could be pursued further, but even a few comments show how the poetic devices used by Racine—antitheses, modifications in rhythm, ambiguity—are all directed towards the dramatic purpose of revealing Néron's psychological reality, as well as suggesting future tragic possibilities in him.

Thus the suggestions here can only be perceived in the context of the play and, whatever the poetic appeal of this passage, it could not be placed in an anthology. In other dramatists, Shakespeare for instance, some speeches, although dramatically relevant, seem to possess an existence of their own because the mood they express coincides with a recognized attitude to a general problem; such is the case with Hamlet's famous soliloquy, 'To be or not to be', or Claudio's speech, 'Ay, but to die...', both of which can be appreciated in themselves as poetic expressions of man's fear of death. There is nothing of the kind in Racine: the lines, if taken out of the play, would lose most, if not all, of their poetic value. Characters in Racine, as we know, do not express moods and general attitudes; they live every minute of a psychological reality which moves constantly and leads them to their doom.

This quality of constant movement, very noticeable in Néron's speech, I have already commented on in a previous chapter when analysing the lifelike characteristic of self-revelation in a Racinian character.[1] What I want to do now is to look more closely at the technical means by which Racine

[1] See chapter 4, pp. 60–65.

achieves this impression of movement and naturalness without losing the formal dignity of his poetic style. This he does by taking advantage of all the possibilities which were latent in the Malherbian alexandrine and in the traditional patterns of rhetoric.[1]

Malherbe's verse could be either stiffly rhetorical or liquidly melodious. The pattern of stiff rhetoric, with repetitions, exclamations, stichomythia, was very useful for translating violence or intellectual argumentation, and Corneille's poetic achievement owes much to it. Racine retains it, but with some significant modifications:

CLYTEMNESTRE   O monstre, que Mégère en ses flancs a porté!
    Monstre, que dans nos bras les enfers ont jeté!
    Quoi! tu ne mourras point? Quoi! pour punir son crime...
    Mais où va ma douleur chercher une victime?
    Quoi! pour noyer les Grecs et leurs mille vaisseaux,
    Mer, tu n'ouvriras pas des abîmes nouveaux?
    Quoi! lorsque les chassant du port qui les recèle,
    L'Aulide aura vomi leur flotte criminelle,
    Les vents, les mêmes vents, si longtemps accusés,
    Ne te couvriront pas de ses vaisseaux brisés?
    Et toi, Soleil, et toi, qui dans cette contrée
    Reconnais l'héritier et le vrai fils d'Atrée,
    Toi, qui n'osas du père éclairer le festin,
    Recule, ils t'ont appris ce funeste chemin.   (v, iv)

There are several rhetorical devices in the passage, exclamation, interrogation, and especially repetition, and these artificial patterns are used most effectively as a stylization of extreme violence. But we immediately note that the total effect produced by the lines rests on a rather complicated combination of these different devices. More important still, the pattern of repetition is not absolutely regular. The interval between the

---

[1] For a long time the importance of traditional rhetoric in Racine attracted little notice. We have now a very thorough and illuminating study by Peter France, *Racine's Rhetoric* (Oxford, 1965).

first two 'Quoi!' is much shorter than between the third and fourth. The rhetorical movement started by the second 'Quoi!' is broken suddenly:

> Quoi! pour punir son crime...
> Mais où va ma douleur...

and remains incomplete. A slightly different pattern of repetition is introduced in 'Les vents, les mêmes vents'; on the other hand in the next lines the repetition of 'toi' recalls the first pattern of the repeated 'Quoi!' but within a shorter space, thus giving an impression of dramatic acceleration. The result of these complications and irregularities is to remove all stiffness from the passage and to prevent it from sounding oratorical in any way. Enough is left of the rhetorical pattern to raise Clytemnestre's wrath and despair to the regal heights of the grand style, but at the same time the violence of the speech is made to appear as a natural disorderly outburst of uncontrolled rage.

Racine also used the liquid melody of the alexandrine. A supple rhythm and the enervating effect of successive vowels produce the well-known musical effect of the lines:

> Ariane, ma sœur! de quel amour blessée,
> Vous mourûtes aux bords où vous fûtes laissée!
>
> (*Phèdre*, I, iii)

Most of Racine's variations in rhythm move between the two examples of vigour and fluidity I have just quoted, so that no definite rhythmical or rhetorical pattern is dominant: patterns melt into one another, producing an overall effect of dignity and naturalness.

While Racine thus succeeds in giving the suppleness of life to the most formal poetic medium without losing its formal beauty, the same miraculous result is again to be found in his use of formal diction and traditional imagery.

The words Racine uses are in themselves colourless, elegantly nondescript, and very limited in number. Even the proper names which appear in his verse—those of the classical gods, biblical names—are, with some rare exceptions, so familiar as to have lost any power of moving the spectators' imagination. Yet the art of Racine seems to prove that any word can assume or recapture a magic power when illuminated by other elements which give it relief, colour and depth.

The simplest illustration of the interaction which gives to a word its former evocative power is one I mentioned in the preceding chapter. The burning passions in the human heart rouse the ancient gods, and the names of Vénus, Minos, Neptune, or even simply the words 'les dieux', carry with them the suggestion of mysterious arbitrariness, eternal power and living presence.

Even words which, like worn-out coins, have no sharpness of relief in themselves are constantly transmuted into the substance of poetry once they are inserted in a pattern or, more exactly, a combination of patterns. In the following lines, which end the speech in which Titus informs Antiochus of his decision to leave Bérénice,

> Adieu: ne quittez point ma princesse, ma reine,
> Tout ce qui de mon cœur fut l'unique désir,
> Tout ce que j'aimerai jusqu'au dernier soupir,　　(III, i)

the rhetorical pattern is clearly perceptible and underlines the characteristic of finality of the two concluding lines. The symmetry in these lines brings out a number of implications, but only in the light of a larger pattern, that of the whole tragedy. It states the parallelism and the opposition between a past 'fut', which appears to be irredeemably over, and a future 'aimerai' of endless duration, while annihilating a present which is for Titus a moment of agonizing hesitation. It suggests the terrifying movement of the pendulum 'toujours'–'jamais' which in *Bérénice* is the very rhythm of suffering, since the tragedy is that of eternal absence and eternal passion. In these two lines, which have powerful resonances, rhetoric is one of the component forces, and the remarkable value assumed here by words which are intrinsically 'unpoetic', a past definite and a future, exists only because of the complexity and the interdependence of the forces at work.

The placing of the word is much more important than the word itself and the same word can undergo subtle alterations in its connotation according to its position. In this respect we may consider Phèdre's lines:

> Ah! cruel, tu m'as trop entendue.
> Je t'en ai dit assez pour te tirer d'erreur.
> Hé bien! connais donc Phèdre et toute sa fureur.
> J'aime. Ne pense pas qu'au moment que je t'aime,
> Innocente à mes yeux je m'approuve moi-même.   (II, v)

The suggestive value of 'tu m'as trop entendue' comes, in the context, from its forceful ambiguity. It translates both Phèdre's bitterness ('you have understood me only too well') and her terror ('you have listened to me for too long'). What is perhaps even more subtle is the effect of the line

> J'aime. Ne pense pas qu'au moment que je t'aime...,

where the same word 'aime' is used twice. The first 'aime', used absolutely, in a kind of frightening isolation, presents Phèdre as the embodiment of passion. For a brief moment she seems to stand in a hieratic attitude, being herself the symbol, even the essence, of all passion. The second 'aime' is a softer echo, a movement from the isolation of her state towards the painful nearness of the object of her love, and a movement which will lead to a desire to explain and retain at least in the eyes of Hippolyte what can be preserved of her moral dignity. But this second 'aime', coming so soon after the first, retains something of the implacable finality of the former and thus carries with it further harmonics all related to the tragic theme of Phèdre's love.

The placing of words so that they should have such harmonics accounts for one more paradox in the Racinian tragedy: the paradoxical nature of a language which is so intellectually clear and yet possesses that opacity made of different layers of meaning which we connect with poetry. Often, when we read poetry, we are aware of the wealth of associations by the kind of obscurity which surrounds a word, an image, a line. In Racine, on the contrary, the meaning of words and sentences, the sequence of thoughts expressed, are perfectly clear. This perfect clarity is, as we know, part of the dramatic technique; it is what makes the characters completely transparent, what enables us to follow every movement of the mechanism which destroys them. But we know also that the dramatic technique of Racine includes other elements, such as specific relations between characters, a special use of time and space, and the use of the historical or legendary side of the heroes; and all these different elements, acting as converging beams focused on the language, give it, beneath the intellectual transparency, disturbing depths and suggestive shadows.

But, whatever the power of suggestion of this poetic language, we must remember that suggestions and associations are strictly limited to their relevance in the dramatic context. And this may compel us to re-assess our reactions to some of Racine's most famous lines.

A line such as

Dans l'Orient désert quel devint mon ennui!

(*Bérénice*, I, iv)

is often mentioned as the perfect expression of the general theme of absence, and compared favourably with another equally well-known line:

Un seul être vous manque et tout est dépeuplé.

What is praised in Racine's line is the exotic flavour of the word 'Orient', conjuring up far-off, mysterious countries, and the effect of understatement produced by 'ennui'. Such appreciation is misdirected: the line is in no way an understatement, as the word 'ennui' had a very strong connotation in the seventeenth century. Moreover, the romantic associations of mystery and exoticism which are attached to the word 'Orient' tend to extend the poetic suggestions of the line much beyond its context.

Undeniably the value of Racine's line lies in the hyperbolical opposition between 'Orient' and 'désert'. The word 'Orient' is both remote and noble, suggesting something larger and more important than a few Eastern states; its importance, as well as its dignified remoteness, increases the negative force of the word 'désert', and the result is a setting for solitude on a vast scale. But the victim of absence, Antiochus, is not dwarfed by this vastness. For him, and for Titus and Bérénice, vast geographical expanses are part of the normal framework of their lives. The word 'Orient' suggests a familiar reality and is a reminder of the responsibility all the heroes in the play have towards the world. Therefore the enlargement which the word conveys is both controlled and enriched by the subjective value it has for Antiochus. There is a great difference in scope and in depth between Lamartine's line, which is a statement in general terms of a general feeling, and Racine's, which translates the inner experience of a given man in a given position.

The right appreciation of Racinian aesthetics requires also that we should discard the distinction that we establish only too easily between 'abstract' and 'concrete' poetry, between the kind of poetry which gives a gnomic form to broad generalizations such as

Rien ne nous rend si grands qu'une grande douleur

and that other kind of poetry which plays on our imagination through references to sensations and concrete objects, of the type: Il est des parfums frais comme des chairs d'enfants.

Racine's poetry does not belong to either category. It cannot be abstract and general since, in conveying the development of the characters' thoughts and feelings, it must give us at every turn the illusion of a particular and unique experience, caught in its most immediate reality. Yet Racine's text includes few concrete words. His poetic language, however, shows that it is not always necessary to use concrete terms to express what we usually associate with a concrete vocabulary: warmth, movement, flexibility, physical pain, shock and vertigo.

We have already seen how a supple handling of the traditional rhetoric enables Racine to recapture the sinuosity and irregularity of human thought. Other elements, too, come into play.

The placing of a word in a conspicuous position, as in the line

Viens voir tous ses attraits, Phœnix, humiliés

(*Andromaque*, II, v)

is not only a subtle revelation of Pyrrhus' inner contradictions: it gives Pyrrhus' mental attitude the pattern of a concrete movement, first upwards, then downwards; and the hiatus in the rhythm between 'attraits' and 'humiliés' has the physical power of a sudden jerk.

More important still is the part played by the context in modifying considerably the connotation of a word. When Roxane, seeing that none of her arguments can move Bajazet, gives up arguing and resolves to punish him, all the intellectual framework of her blackmail and her threats suddenly collapses and only desperate passion remains:

Bajazet, écoutez, je sens que je vous aime. (II, i)

The word 'sens' is neither abstract nor concrete, or perhaps is both. Our usual distinctions do not work here. 'Sens' may be abstract to a certain extent, since it means 'I realize that I love you', but, because it is placed at the precise point where there are no arguments left, no possible resort to the intellect, the word expresses something which is almost pure sensation, a burning pang obliterating the whole field of consciousness.

In a similar way Racine, like Malherbe or Bossuet, knows the strange physical power which some abstract terms can possess, words which are potentially impressive because of their characteristic of absoluteness, like 'toujours', 'jamais', 'rien', 'tout', 'éternité', 'néant', etc. Here again the effect depends on complex relations, not only between a line and its context, but also between several lines which, coming in succession, influence one another.

Thus when Roxane reminds Bajazet

> Que j'ai sur votre vie un empire suprême,
> Que vous ne respirez qu'autant que je vous aime?　(II, i)

the full impact of the first line, which is an abstract statement couched in conventional terms, and of its sinister connotation, is only felt with the second line, where the intimate and threatening coupling of 'respirez' and 'aime' reduces the physical reality of Bajazet into a sort of emanation of Roxane's will. We realize the terrifying bond between the two characters, the vicarious and precarious nature of Bajazet's existence, and are almost ready for the horrifying implications of the last lines of the speech—

> Et sans ce même amour, qu'offensent vos refus,
> Songez-vous, en un mot, que vous ne seriez plus?

—and yet the lines open up a kind of abyss. The very abstractness of 'que vous ne seriez plus' is more frightening than any mention of death or of a corpse. This vertiginous effect lingers on through the next lines spoken by Roxane and gives an intense emotional value to the line

> Rentre dans le néant dont je t'ai fait sortir,

with the word 'néant' resounding, like a final chord, like a louder echo containing all the harmonics of horror.

Since the achievement of this kind of poetry is based on

relations and correlations and since the possibilities of combining various elements are unlimited, only a small number of words is needed to translate every nuance required by the tragic pattern of the play; and, although all the characters speak the same language, it is even possible for Racine to individualize, to a certain extent, the way in which his heroes express themselves.

The violent clash of words in the line

> J'entendrai des regards que vous croirez muets;
> > *(Britannicus, II, iii)*

the cruel sharpness produced by the startling alliance 'entendrai'–'regards'–'muets', the tone of brutality, arrogance and boasting, can only belong to Néron.

The line spoken by Xipharès,

> Je vous rappelle un songe effacé de votre âme, (I, ii)

reflects the extreme gentleness, verging on shyness, and the refined courtesy which characterize the passionate love of Xipharès and Monime. The graceful and melancholy effect of the line is due not only to its even melody but also to some subtle interaction of the words 'songe', 'effacé', 'âme'. Xipharès, who does not know that Monime loves him, claims only to conjure up a past event (their first meeting) which presumably has for her no more reality than a dream. The deprecatory tone is rendered almost magically: the word 'effacé' increases the unreality of the event and at the same time the dignified vagueness of the words 'songe' and 'âme' is both enhanced and made more substantial by the semi-physical and elusive image of some delicate obliteration.

There remains Racine's use of imagery; and once more we must push aside our modern preconceptions concerning the value of images. We usually expect a good image to be original, striking and personal to the author. Racine's images are traditional, unobtrusive and public property. This is in keeping with the aesthetics of the Renaissance, which is still the aesthetics of the seventeenth century. The decorative value of the image was derived from the dignified and precious patina given by tradition. Its function was intellectual: what was expected from a good image was that it should be clearly significant of a quality in the experience chosen by the poet. The achievement depended therefore on the aptness of the image and on its degree of significance.

In Racine the power of significance of the image is immensely increased by its position in a complex network of interdependent elements. This is why the famous line of Pyrrhus—

Brûlé de plus de feux que je n'en allumai

(*Andromaque*, I, iv)

—is not just a witty conceit, as has sometimes been said, but possesses an intense poetic value. I have already mentioned the dramatic implications which the line includes in its context. 'Brûlé de plus de feux' is not an overstatement in the case of a hero who is destroyed by his passion, nor are the fires of Troy a convenient recollection of past exploits: they are a constant reminder of what separates for ever Pyrrhus and Andromaque. Moreover, through the conceit we perceive the poetic justice which strikes at Pyrrhus and, what is even more tragic, his mistaken belief that the violence of his love more than compensates for the violence of his past actions.

There are key images in some of the tragedies, recurring time and time again and as such becoming symbols, although the latter term should be used with some care. These recurrent images do not constitute a symbolic structure transcending the text. Their symbolic value exists only in the context of the play. One of the most interesting of these key images is that of daylight in *Phèdre*. The value of this image is that it is related to so many elements in the play: to the use made of space, the effect of a vast open sky, the dazzling unchanging light of the day; to Hippolyte's innocence; to moral order, so that it takes on its

complexity of significance from the complexity of Phèdre's reactions to light: fear, adoration, feeling of agoraphobia, envy,
moral respect. Its decorative quality is traditional but particularly relevant here, as the worship of daylight was a Greek concept.
It suggests, in a delicately sensuous way, a Greek atmosphere
without in any way suggesting a landscape. Its greatest quality
is perhaps to be unobtrusive, the more so as it can hide
itself so easily, the word 'jour' meaning both day and daylight,
and because the full effect of the symbol depends also on its
correlation with other words as unobtrusive as itself, such as
'lumière', 'clair', 'ciel', 'serein', 'clarté', which are linked with
the same connotations.

The great poetic beauty of Hippolyte's well-known line—

Le jour n'est pas plus pur que le fond de mon cœur (IV, ii)

—is too often explained away by the melodious succession of
the vowel sounds it contains. Certainly the quiet rhythm of the
line with its even stresses produced by the succession of mono-
syllables gives a kind of firm simplicity to Hippolyte's statement. In his desperate situation of being unfairly accused by his
father, the strongest argument can be only a statement. Innocence cannot be proved, it ought to be a self-evident reality,
as obvious as the light of day. 'Le fond de mon cœur' is an
ordinary, rather abstract, expression, but all the associations
which the words 'jour' and 'pur' derive from their relationship with the central image of daylight come to increase the
significance of the statement. The image satisfies by its perfect
aptness: Hippolyte *is* innocence and *is* daylight. At the same
time, through this line, this inner quality of the character—
in fact 'le fond de mon cœur'—seems to be made of a precious substance, as luminous, as impalpable, and as limitless as
all the light which composes our mental picture of a clear
sky.

But perhaps the most beautiful quality of this image of daylight is the way in which it appears for the last time in the last

words spoken by Phèdre, gathering together all the implications it has conveyed throughout the play and then dissolving
in a kind of apotheosis.

It is sometimes necessary for Racine to thicken the substance
of his imagery, to underline the key words. The poetic atmosphere in *Athalie* forms a contrast with the particular transparency
found in *Phèdre*, and is dictated by the parallelism between the
tragic pattern and the pattern of Christian order. The poetry of
the chorus is that of Racine's religious lyrics and fits admirably
with the impersonal fervour, the graceful serenity, of a Christian
moral order. Although the metre is lighter than the alexandrine
and the images slightly different from what they are elsewhere,
the choruses do not clash with the rest of the play. The diction
and the images (which are traditional) are ruled by the same
principles of aesthetics as the speeches of the protagonists. Moreover, the delicacy of rhythm and the subtle use of acknowledged
poetic diction, as in the stanza

> Tel en un secret vallon,
> Sur le bord d'une onde pure,
> Croît à l'abri de l'aquilon
> Un jeune lis, l'amour de la nature, (II, ix)

are related to other elements in the play which also express the
virtues of a Christian order, such as the innocence of the children
and the gentle faith of Josabet.

In contrast, the tragic pattern centred on the idea of a cruel
God and of destructive passions shows in the darkest colours.
The word 'sang' recurs constantly, so does the mention of wild
beasts or savage animals, dogs, lions, bears, wolves. References
to metals—

> Comment en un plomb vil l'or pur s'est-il changé?
> (III, vii)

—contribute to the rich barbaric setting of the play, still more
emphasized by allusions to the ritual ceremonies in the Temple.
Whereas in the choruses biblical names assume a quiet serenity,

they sound startlingly strange and terrifying in the mouth of the angry Joad. From Malherbe, even from an older tradition, Racine has borrowed the impressive effect of some sonorous proper names, as in the lines in which Joad attacks Mathan:

> Sors donc de devant moi, monstre d'impiété.
> De toutes tes horreurs, va, comble la mesure.
> Dieu s'apprête à te joindre à la race parjure,
> Abiron et Dathan, Doëg, Achitophel. (III, v)

Athalie may appear more obviously poetic than the other tragedies of Racine. Yet basically it is the same poetic technique. The most terrifying effects, which are to be found particularly in passages where the tragic pattern and moral order become inextricably mixed, are produced by the art with which Racine, as we have seen, can use the most abstract words, the most negative statements:

> Si quelque transgresseur enfreint cette promesse,
> Qu'il éprouve, grand Dieu, ta fureur vengeresse:
> Qu'avec lui ses enfants, de ton partage exclus,
> Soient au rang de ces morts que tu ne connais plus. (IV, iii)

The sinister horror of this curse, which in the manner of the Old Testament includes the next generations in the punishment at the hands of a revengeful God, is brought about not by the words 'ces morts' only but by the dark negativeness of 'que tu ne connais plus'.

★

A study of Racinian tragedy necessarily begins and ends with the language of the plays. It is through our first immediate reaction to a single line taken at random that we discover how much Racine can move us. It is when any line of Racine can reveal to us its complete significance, that is, all its connections with all the other elements of the tragedy, that we appreciate Racine fully.

Perhaps, as a test, the reader might go back to Phèdre's last speech, which I have mentioned several times in the course of this study, and find in it the different facets of what is a single diamond: the relevance of time and space; the ineluctable destruction of the heroine through the arbitrariness of passion and of the gods; the double and paradoxical aspects of the Racinian protagonist, so transparent and yet so present physically, so near and yet so removed; the interaction of the tragic pattern and the moral order; the place of the speech in the structure of the play; the use of words, rhetoric, and images. But perfect appreciation should have the same miraculous quality as that of Racine's own achievement: the different elements I have enumerated as well as the multiple connections between them should be perceived at once, separately and jointly, in the same moment as we experience the disturbing and supremely satisfactory beauty of the lines.

APPENDIX

VISTAS IN RACINIAN CRITICISM

This is not a survey of the critical works which have been devoted to Racine, or even an *état présent* of Racinian studies, but a brief comment on a few conspicuous trends in contemporary criticism which are particularly interesting because they illustrate the difficulties encountered by the modern reader when approaching Racinian tragedy.

Racine's greatness, if it is to be asserted once more by the twentieth century, seems to require particular interpretations destined to adapt the dramatist's works to the taste of our age, and especially to certain preconceived ideas about what literature in general and poetic drama in particular should be.

Romanticism still lingers on, and accordingly the criteria chosen by some critics to appreciate the value of the tragic or the poetic element in Racine are romantic criteria.

To begin with, the basically neutral quality of Racine's poetic instrument is not always appreciated. Whatever the prosodic perfection and the melody of the Racinian alexandrine, it has appeared rather flat and colourless, and ingenious efforts have been made to swell its musical overtones and to bring its pattern into sharper relief. In a recent book,[1] the rhymes are considered as having an importance and a life of their own; separated from the rest of the line, then inflated with thematic connotations, they constitute, through a complicated interplay of sound effects, a symbolic orchestration. Another critic, Pierre Guéguen,[2] had already attempted to extract from the musical element in Racine all the suggestions and associations which the very sound of a word may possess according to the wildest theories of nineteenth- and twentieth-century 'phonaes-

---

[1] Marcelle Blum, *Le Thème symbolique dans le théâtre de Racine* (2 vols., Paris, 1962–5).   [2] *La Poésie de Racine* (Paris, 1946).

thetics'. The Racinian text becomes a sound-picture which, in an immediate and magic way, reveals to the audience the tragic implications of every line. For instance, for M. Guéguen, there is no need for the spectators to know anything about Minos or Pasiphaé in order to appreciate the famous line

La fille de Minos et de Pasiphaé,

since 'la peinture sonore nous renseigne que ce sont parents insolites, monstrueux; ce Minos au visage de syllabes si graves, cette Pasiphaé au nom si mouvementé. Racine ne dit pas, "Juge aux Enfers, nymphe docile aux taureaux"; il le suggère musicalement.'[1]

This musical symbolism is only one aspect of a more general trend towards finding a symbolic interpretation for every aspect of the Racinian tragedy. We have been told, ever since Baudelaire, that the world is a 'forêt de symboles' and that poetry, in order to move us, must suggest a universe of mysteries far beyond the human condition. Therefore the various elements of Racine's tragedies, and mostly the images, are made to signify a larger poetic vision which may well appear to the non-initiated completely alien to the tragedy under discussion. Thus M. Guéguen focuses Racine's poetic universe on the great themes of the elements: water, earth, air, fire; and studies with delight Racine's 'nautical tragedies'. For a more recent critic, Roland Barthes,[2] the central image in *Phèdre* is Earth. It is interesting to note here how the quest for symbols is pursued with more and more subtlety as time goes on, for M. Barthes does not choose what is obviously the key image in the play: daylight. The less evident the symbol, the greater its value. The supreme achievement of this kind of approach would be, it seems, to discover beneath the Racinian alexandrines an understructure of hidden layers embodying the doctrines of the Rosicrucians.

[1] *Ibid.* p. 18.   [2] *Sur Racine* (Paris, 1960), pp. 119, 120.

So far it has not been possible to excavate beneath the text in search of esoteric revaluation. Meanwhile, it has appeared more rewarding, as well as much easier, to resort to other techniques in order to endow the Racinian tragedy with that metaphysical quality without which some modern sensibilities cannot react strongly to any form of literature. It seems that the requirement of any literary work is that it should express some intimation of a supernatural world or admit of a philosophical interpretation. A tragic universe based on the destructive force of the passions, working within a purely human context, is thought too limited to justify a genuine admiration for Racine. With the help of phonology, sociology, symbolism, or at times nothing more than the contagious enthusiasm of wishful thinking, a number of critics have done their best to convince the twentieth-century spectator that he can find in Racinian tragedy his own spiritual longings, his hankering after the Absolute, his questioning of his relationship with God—in short, what, since Madame de Staël, have been some of the prominent features of romantic literature. The very titles of some of the critical works on Racine are significant in themselves: *Le Dieu caché*, by Lucien Goldmann, and the sub-title of one of the two volumes Marcelle Blum devotes to the symbolism of the rhymes, *Du psychologique au divin*. Equally significant is the use of philosophical terms in M. Barthes's comments: '*Phèdre* est une tragédie nominaliste', as well as the use of capital letters for words such as 'Existence', 'Etre', 'Bien', 'Mal', so as to give them an extra metaphysical dimension.

One more romantic criterion has still to be mentioned: the subjective quality of the work. On this point, too, contemporary criticism goes very far at times. Biographical criticism, *à la* Sainte-Beuve, is not considered sufficient. Except for Racine's Jansenist upbringing, which is retained because it serves also towards a religious interpretation for Racinian tragedy, the other events of the dramatist's life are often judged disappointing. Subjective value must emerge through rich evidence drawn from the innermost parts of the writer's personality. Therefore, after the hidden God, betrayed by his absence, we meet the hidden self, revealed by frustration. The works of M. Mauron[1] and M. Baudoin[2] muster the modern tools of psycho-analysis to lay bare the secrets concealed in Racine's metaphors. Besides, for the romantic imagination, the subconscious mind possesses in itself a poetic quality. Psycho-analysis gives a scientific basis to a kind of Nervalian universe, made up of mysterious associations, of a complex network of *correspondances*, of entrancing correlations with the distant past of man, even with primitive eras. There is here the possibility of adding a whole gamut of symbolic harmonics to former symbolist interpretations. The metaphor of 'feux', for instance, is not only made more poetic by a connection with one of the four elements in nature; it is also given an added flavour by its supposed link with Racine's obsession with burning things and an even more extended evocative power by bringing into it some of the general considerations of psycho-analysis on the element of fire.[3]

If we consider together these critical trends, we notice that all these interpretations of Racine are centrifugal; starting from the text, they draw round it a succession of rings which move further and further away from it. The rhymes break loose from the prosodic pattern, sound-waves extend as far as the imagination can go, tragic themes and images expand and get lost in the subconscious, the great force of nature, divine arcana, or pre-history.

This attempt at modernizing Racinian tragedy, however seductive it appears to contemporary tastes, should, in my opinion, be firmly resisted. We possess enough literary master-

---

[1] Charles Mauron, *L'inconscient dans l'œuvre et la vie de Racine* (Gap, 1957).
[2] Charles Baudoin, *Jean Racine, l'enfant du Désert* (Paris, 1963).
[3] Cf. *ibid.* pp. 47–54.

pieces which are magnificent expressions of the romantic or post-romantic world vision, and have no need to compel earlier works to fit in with the prevalent and temporary mood of our age. The critical tendencies I have mentioned are unsatisfactory in several ways. They are obviously anachronistic, as they show clearly a conscious or unconscious refusal to consider Racine in the light of seventeenth-century aesthetics. Even if one questions the permanence of such criteria for the value of a literary work and claims the critic's right to an interpretation in keeping with his own times (anachronism considered as one of the fine arts, which is M. Barthes's critical position), the results obtained by such an approach have so far been disappointing. One basic necessity remains for the critic; that of putting forward a coherent and complete interpretation of a work. This is what the critical studies I have mentioned fail to do. It is hardly surprising. Dismembering Racinian tragedy, they tend to focus on one aspect while ignoring the others, and can therefore in no way account for that perfection and relevance of structure which are the hallmark of any masterpiece and which even the most superficial reader of Racine can feel to be present in the dramatist's works.

On the other hand, some books among those discussed in this chapter have their own interest, although not as literary criticism. Biography is both a science and an art in its own right. It is a justifiable curiosity to be interested in Racine, the man, as in any other important historical figure. The text of his works may throw some light on his personality; one might want to know, for instance, whether Racine's beliefs coincided with those which he took into account to establish the pattern of moral order. The question is irrelevant for the literary critic, who need not even decide to what extent Racine was conscious or not of conforming to contemporary values, but relevant to the biographer. A work such as M. Mauron's book belongs more to biography than to literary criticism and is also an important contribution to a field of research which is primarily concerned with psychological rather than literary values. The literary critic's interest lies in the finished product of the creative mind. As to the very complex processes which take place in the mind of the author while he composes his writings, they certainly constitute a fascinating problem, which might well be considered as belonging to psychological studies.

The sociological approach of M. Goldmann raises another question. I personally am very much in agreement with him as to the importance of what he calls 'the collective consciousness' in the work of an individual writer. The pattern of order in Racine rests on the moral, political and religious values which were those of his age. Moreover, if the tragic pattern in Racine is centred on human passions, it is, as I said, because a strong interest in man's passions was a feature of the 'collective consciousness' of the seventeenth century. The stress on passions may have had a Jansenist origin; the problem is in fact more complicated, and Jansenism itself may well be no more than the most conspicuous expression of a split between religious life and earthly values which turned the seventeenth century into a two-truth world. To account for the secularization of literature in the seventeenth century (with the exception of writers such as Pascal and Bossuet who were concerned with one of the two truths, religion) is undoubtedly a very interesting problem. The fact remains that Racine's tragedies belong to secularized literature, to the world of the other truth, the moralist's world. The objectivity of M. Goldmann's scientific approach breaks down because his remarkable documentation of Racine's own times is made to serve a conception of tragedy which is very much in keeping with modern tendencies and has little to do with the seventeenth century. Moreover, a really scientific and objective study would have taken into account not only the phenomenon of 'moralism' in literature but also seventeenth-century dramatic conventions. The discrepancy to be found in this critical

work between the scientific principles and a certain conditioning imposed by twentieth-century tendencies may well be
explained by those same critical methods of the author himself,
and sociological criticism could be fruitfully applied to M.
Goldmann's book.

*

It is obviously very difficult to avoid altogether subjective reactions to Racine's works. This does not greatly matter so long
as the subjective characteristics of such reactions are honestly
realized. No criteria are eternal, nor is human nature, but it is
worth appreciating Racinian tragedy in the light of the aesthetics which were necessarily those of Racine. The limitations
set by the moralists to the significance of their works are, moreover, an asset when it comes to comparatively long survival.
Our interest in human passions as seen within the human condition is likely to outlive many of the romantic dreams. As for
the effort required to understand and enjoy a work according to
aesthetic conventions which differ slightly from those to which
we are used, it is well to remember that no great work of
literature is easy. Going back to past traditions which are not so
very far from us is no hardship. It is not the pedantry of a
historian but simply the acknowledgement of that precious
value for any civilized man: culture.

SELECT BIBLIOGRAPHY

The bibliography of Racine is so rich and varied that it is not easy to make a choice and I regretfully have to omit excellent articles and some most interesting books. The following list claims to do no more than mention a few works which are particularly relevant to the problems discussed in the present study.

FACTUAL AND GENERAL CRITICISM

Knight, R. C., *Racine et la Grèce*, Paris, 1950.
Picard, R., *La Carrière de Jean Racine*, Paris, 1956.
Pommier, J., *Aspects de Racine*, Paris, 1954.
Scherer, J., *La dramaturgie classique en France*, Paris, 1950.

CRITICISM MORE ESPECIALLY CONCERNED WITH THE DRAMATIC STRUCTURE AND AESTHETIC VALUE OF RACINIAN TRAGEDY

France, P., *Racine's Rhetoric*, Oxford, 1965.
Giraudoux, J., *Racine*, Paris, 1929.
Lapp, J. C., *Aspects of Racinian Tragedy*, Toronto, 1956.
Maulnier, T., *Racine*, Paris, 1936.
May, G., *Tragédie cornélienne, tragédie racinienne* (Illinois Studies in Language and Literature, vol. XXXII), Illinois, 1948.
Picard, R., Introductions to the plays in the Pléiade edition of *Œuvres complètes de Racine*, Paris, 1950.
Vinaver, E., *Racine et la Poésie tragique*, Paris, 1951. (English translation by P. Mansell Jones: *Racine and Poetic Tragedy*, Manchester, 1955.)
Weinberg, B., *The Art of Jean Racine*, Chicago, 1963.

CRITICISM STRONGLY INFLUENCED BY THE CRITERIA DISCUSSED IN THE APPENDIX

Barthes, R., *Sur Racine*, Paris, 1960.
Blum, Marcelle, *Le Thème symbolique dans le théâtre de Racine*, 2 vols., Paris, 1962 and 1965.
Guéguen, P., *La Poésie de Racine*, Paris, 1946.

Goldmann, L., *Le Dieu caché*, Paris, 1955.

—— *Jean Racine, dramaturge*, Collection des grands dramaturges, Paris, 1956.

> The latter is a condensed version on the views of Racinian tragedy expressed in the previous work.

Hubert, J. D., *Essai d'exégèse racinienne: Les Secrets témoins*, Paris, 1956.

> Contains remarkable analyses which keep their interest even for the reader who does not share the author's views.

Mauron, C., *L'inconscient dans l'œuvre et la vie de Racine*, Annales de la Faculté de Lettres d'Aix, Gap, 1957.

INDEX